NATURE AND UNDERSTANDING

Nature and Understanding

The Metaphysics and Method of Science

NICHOLAS RESCHER

CLARENDON PRESS · OXFORD
2000

OXFORD
UNIVERSITY PRESS

Great Clarendon Street, Oxford OX2 6DP

Oxford University Press is a department of the University of Oxford.
It furthers the University's objective of excellence in research, scholarship,
and education by publishing worldwide in

Oxford New York

Athens Auckland Bangkok Bogotá Buenos Aires Calcutta
Cape Town Chennai Dar es Salaam Delhi Florence Hong Kong Istanbul
Karachi Kuala Lumpur Madrid Melbourne Mexico City Mumbai
Nairobi Paris São Paulo Shanghai Singapore Taipei Tokyo Toronto Warsaw

and associated companies in Berlin Ibadan

Oxford is a registered trade mark of Oxford University Press
in the UK and certain other countries

Published in the United States
by Oxford University Press Inc., New York

British Library Cataloguing in Publication Data
Data available

Library of Congress Cataloging in Publication Data
Data available
ISBN 0–19–825085–1

1 3 5 7 9 10 8 6 4 2

Typeset in Minion
by Kolam Information Services Pvt. Ltd, Pondicherry, India
Printed in Great Britain by
Biddles Ltd
Guildford and King's Lynn

Preface

In his magnum opus entitled *Philosophia prima sive ontologia*,[1] the eminent German philosopher Christian Wolff (1679–1750) devoted considerable attention to such generic features of reality as the order and structure of nature's things. Here, as was typical in the earlier era of what Kant characterized as dogmatic philosophy, the fundamental features of the real were thought of in ontological and transcendental terms of reference. Indeed Kant himself still thought of them as a priori and thereby necessary, although he shifted the responsibility for this circumstance to the constitution of the human intellect itself. With the more thoroughgoing naturalization of philosophy in the post-Kantian era, such issues came to be regarded as having to hinge upon the findings of the sciences. But there remains the interesting and still largely unexplored prospect of assessing what light can be shed on reality by examining the *modus operandi* of natural science itself, focusing as much on its findings as on its conceptual and methodological presuppositions.

There thus looms before us the prospect of looking from a scientific point of view at such central ideas of traditional metaphysics as the simplicity of nature, its comprehensibility, or its systemic integrity. This is a theme to which I have devoted a series of diversified publications extending over thirty years. The present book seeks to synthesize and co-ordinate the fruits of these inquiries and to describe—in a way accessible to philosophers and non-philosophers alike—the metaphysical situation that characterizes the process of inquiry in natural science.

I am grateful to Estelle Burris for the patient and competent way in which she has managed to bring this material into a form suitable for the printer's needs, despite various obstacles, not least among which is my distinctly unsatisfactory handwriting. I am also appreciative of the generous and able editorial help of Peter Momtchiloff.

N.R.

Pittsburgh, Pa.
December 1999

---

[1] The most recent and best edition of this work is that of Jean École (Joannes Ecole) (Darmstadt: Wissenschaftliche Buchgesellschaft, 1962).

Contents

Contents   ix

List of Figures

Introduction

Metaphysical Principles in Erotetic Perspective

Metaphysics seeks to answer our most fundamental and far-reaching questions about the ways of the world. The discipline, as traditionally conceived, deals with existence at the most general level of the very possibility of knowledge. Its concern is with the features of all existence—natural and artificial alike—that underpin the prospects of knowledge, and it seeks to set out the fundamentals of our understanding of the real. Its characteristic task is to deal at a very general and inclusive level with our questions about the world and our prospects for resolving them.

From its very inception in classical antiquity, metaphysics has been conceived of as including 'ontology', the study of the nature of existence and of the kinds or categories of things there are, determining the natural groupings involved, their interrelationships, their reasons for being, and their most pervasive or most fundamental features.

Now erotetics, the theory of questions, includes among other things the issue of classification. And it is clear that questions in general can be classified in various ways. Their mode of formulation offers the most immediate prospect, and the resultant typology would run as follows:

- *Why* questions ('Why is condition *C* realized?')
- *When* questions ('When is condition *C* realized?')
- *Where* questions ('Where is condition *C* realized?')
- *How* questions ('How does condition *C* come to be realized?')
- *Is-it-true* questions ('Is condition *C* realized?')
- *Is-it-possible* questions ('Can condition *C* be realized?')
- *What if* questions ('What ensues if condition *C* is realized?')
- and so on.

Such a classification provides a very general and abstract taxonomy of questions according to their form rather than their specific subject-matter content. And it is exactly the generic issues which arise here that define the agenda of metaphysics. Metaphysics inquires into the prospects of grasping the why, when, how, etc. of things, of actuality and possibility and so on.

A general analysis of the situation shows that *all questions have presuppositions.* And in fact there is one common sort of presupposition that any question Q whatsoever has, namely, 'There is an answer to Q.' That is to say every question presupposes that it has an answer.[1]

Additionally, however, the questions of any taxonomic type *T* share the broader presupposition, 'There are, in general, answers to questions of the type to which I belong.' Such a generic presupposition of tractability is a schematic fact about questions in general. It constitutes the Fundamental Presupposition of all question-answering endeavour that questions generally share a common commitment to the presupposition schema: 'Questions of my type generally have answers.' And metaphysical questions are no exception to this rule.

Specifically in the context of the indicated mode-of-formulation question typology the Fundamental Presupposition yields the following principles:

1. *Why* questions: 'All why questions regarding the world's occurrences have answers.' That is: with regard to why questions some appropriate answer will in general be forthcoming. For facts about the world there is, in general, a cogent reason why. (This, in effect, is the traditional metaphysical Principle of Sufficient Reason.)

2. *When* questions and *where* questions. 'For any when or where question about situations in nature there will in general be an answer forthcoming by way of a space–time placement with regard to the condition that is in question.' Again we have here a fundamental principle of metaphysics: that real events, occurrences, and states of affairs invariably have a placement within the space–time framework. (This is simply the metaphysical thesis of the spatiotemporal character of what is real in nature.)

3. *How* questions. 'All how questions regarding natural processes have an answer.' The metaphysical principle that nature has a *modus operandi*, that there is always a definite way-and-manner for occurrences. (This is the metaphysical principle of order, insisting that nature's *modus operandi* is systematic: the world is a cosmos.)

4. *How-come* questions. Such questions ask: 'How did it come about that such-and-such a state of affairs obtains?' They are subject

---

[1] For further details regarding presupposition see the author's *Empirical Inquiry* (Totowa, NJ: Rowman Littlefield, 1982).

to the idea that: 'Nature is pervasively governed by causal processes so that such explanatory questions always have an answer.' A Principle of Causality obtains.

5. *Is-it-true* questions. 'Any given specification regarding nature either does or does not obtain.' (This is the Law of Excluded Middle in its metaphysical guise.)

6. *Is it possible* questions. Such questions too are always answerable: 'There is, all-pervasively, a definite demarcation line that separates what is possible from what is not—what can and what cannot happen.' 'Otherwise imaginable possibilities are always either authentically possible or not: there is no middle ground here with the possible, any more than there is with the actual.' A Principle of Explicability obtains to assure the rationality of the real.

Such considerations bring a noteworthy realization to light, namely that there is a unified and systemic explanatory rationale to the cardinal governing principles of traditional metaphysics. It stands as follows:

> The key principles of traditional metaphysics are no more—and no less—than *pre*suppositions assuring that the main types of questions about the world can, in principle, be answered.

This is to say that those metaphysical principles provide the inquiry-facilitating for the main taxonomic types of substantive questions we have about things.

On this basis, the route of question-presupposition analysis leads to such principles of traditional metaphysics as

- Uniformity and orderliness of nature: the world as a cosmos. (Item 3)
- Intelligibility of nature. (Item 1)
- Rationality of nature. (Item 6)
- Definiteness of nature. (Item 5)
- Lawfulness of nature (as a system with a definite *modus operandi*). A Principle of Causality obtains: all of nature's eventuations transpire under the aegis of causal principles. (Item 4)
- Spatiotemporality of nature (any real occurrence takes place in space and time). (Item 2)

These considerations indicate that those traditional metaphysical principles are not learned facts that we derive from our scientific examination of nature. They are not parts of empirical science as such. Instead, they are presuppositions to which we subscribe because we require them to make the empirical study of natural reality feasible as a rational project. What we have in this sector of metaphysics is not a matter of substantive answers to our substantive questions about the world—not facts that we take away from the study of nature—but rather *sine-qua-non* conditions for the answerability of the major mode-of-formulation types of substantive questions that can be raised.

Metaphysical issues are thus 'basic' or 'fundamental' because they are the product of a methodological stance that facilitates empirical inquiry rather than being a product of our observational study of nature. What those principles of traditional metaphysics do is to provide the question-generic presuppositions of factual inquiry. Natural science (physics, as the Greeks called it) provides the specific answers to our specific questions. But metaphysics is a matter of 'first principles': it sets out the presuppositional framework within which those answers are developed.

Accordingly validation in metaphysics is not empirical (observational) but functional (presuppositional)—at any rate in the first instance. For in the final analysis, to be sure, the success of the inquiries that are conducted under their aegis provides some retrospective revalidation for the step of having subscribed to their presuppositions in the first place. On this basis, those postulations that are represented by the basic metaphysical principles that we presuppose are ultimately in principle defeasible. If the prospect of inquiry based upon them were to issue in abject failure, this would of course indicate the untenability of those principles. What would thus ensue would be a pragmatic invalidation owing to the retrospective consideration that reliance on such principles 'just did not work out'. But the successful development of physics—in the Greek sense of the term—shows that there is in fact no real danger of this.

One of the key tasks of metaphysics—perhaps not its only task but certainly one of its principal ones—is thus to give us an account not of what natural science maintains, but rather how it is that we are in a position to provide such an account at all. The cardinal aim of the enterprise is to enable us to understand how it is that we humans, circumstanced as we are and proceeding in the way we do, are able to devise a reliable account of the *modus operandi* of the world we live in.

But there is yet another aspect of the matter. Presuppositional inquiry in relation to science has two aspects, depending on whether we ask, 'What presuppositions are called for if we are to do science *at all*?' or 'What presuppositions are called for if we are to do science in the particular way in which the course of experience has ultimately taught us to proceed?' Those initial most fundamental principles are fixed. But then less fundamental implementation is something else again, something learned, something in relation to what the case of experience costs. At this less fundamental level the presuppositions and methodological principles of natural science must be retrospectively informed and restructured in the light of the deliverance of scientific agency itself. (At this stage we can usefully resort to Otto Neurath's graphic image of the boat refitted and repaired while sailing in the open sea.) At this level of consideration metaphysics not merely underpins but also reflects science.

Does such an approach reduce metaphysics to natural science? Not really! Scientific knowledge is a matter of securing descriptive theses about the world's *modus operandi* by means of *observation-based evidentiation*. Metaphysics, by contrast, is a matter of elucidating the presuppositional backyard of such knowledge by means of *second-order reflection*. The one answers questions about the descriptive make-up of the real. The other addresses higher-order questions about the accessibility and the nature of such knowledge. Both are indeed connected with systematizing the world's facts. But the nature of the connection is very different, relying in the one case on *evidential* systemization and on the other on *reflective* systemization.

So much, then, for the inherent nature and the justifactory basis of metaphysical principles—their rooting in our questions about the world. The issue of their implications and broader ramifications and interconnections remains. And it is against this background that the aims of the present deliberations take form. It is seen as a given that such information as we have about the world is provided by our scientific knowledge of its nature. But the discussion proceeds in the recognition that behind or alongside science there also lies the question of what features of the world must be accepted through the very fact that our scientific information about it arises in the way that we find it does.

The deliberations of the book will thus consider the intricacies of reciprocal interrelationships between reality and our knowledge of it with a view to elucidating some general structural and theoretical

1

The Systematicity of Nature

SYNOPSIS

(1) Cognitive and ontological systematicity are two aspects of this conception, the former relating to the make-up of our information about nature, the latter to that of the world itself. (2) The Principle of Least Effort affords a rationale for the simplicity preference crucial for cognitive systematicity. (3) Economy is an inherent aspect of rationality. (4) But this does not prejudge the ontological issue of nature's make-up. (5) It must, however, be acknowledged that (a reasonable degree of) ontological systematicity is a causal requisite for ever carrying on a successful process of inquiry. A world that is insufficiently systematic and verges on chaos cannot provide an environment within which any learning is possible. (6) And, exactly because (a fair degree of) ontological systematicity is required for successful inquiry, cognitive systematicity is the best index that we have of the world's ontological systematicity. Moreover, the fact that our inquiry process is based on a methodological commitment to cognitive systematicity will not prevent our discovering the extent—whatever it be—of the world's complexity or even disorder.

1.1. Cognitive and Ontological Systematicity

The ideal of developing our knowledge scientifically stands co-ordinate with the idea of system. Now the conception of a system has historically been applied both to objects in the world and to bodies of knowledge. In the face of this ambivalence, it is important to distinguish between the ontological systematicity (simplicity, coherence, regularity, uniformity, etc.) of the objects of our knowledge—that is, between systematicity as a feature of things—and the cognitive systematicity of our (putative) knowledge or information about things.

In fact, three significantly distinguishable roles must be assigned to systematicity:

I. Cognitive Systematicity

1. *Codificational systematicity*—systematicity as a feature of the organization of our knowledge.
2. *Criterial systematicity*—systematicity as a criterial standard for assessing the acceptability of theses.

II. Non-Cognitive (Ontological) Systematicity

3. *Ontological systematicity*—systematicity as a descriptive characteristic of objects—in principle including the whole of the natural universe.

Given this distinction of several modes of systematicity there arises the question of their relative fundamentality. Pre-eminently we must ask: is systematicity at bottom an epistemic desideratum for our knowledge regarding nature or an ontologically descriptive feature of nature itself?

From the epistemic standpoint, the parameters of systematicity—simplicity, coherence, regularity, etc.—can effectively serve to regulate and control the claims of our explanatory-descriptive accounts of the world to rational acceptability. In particular, they can serve as *regulative principles of inquiry*, as instruments for assessing appropriateness and acceptability in the conduct of our cognitive endeavours. If a characterization of the workings of nature manifested a substantial lack of cognitive systematization, it would thereby betoken its own inadequacy. One could not rationally rest content with such an account because, by hypothesis, it contravenes what is in fact a characterizing condition of an *adequate* account.

But this perspective on cognitive systematicity is not the whole of the story.

1.2. The Principle of Least Effort and the Methodological Status of Simplicity-Preference in Science

In the days of the medieval schoolmen and of those later rationalistic philosophers whom Kant was wont to characterize as dogmatists, simplicity was viewed as an *ontological feature* of the world. Just as it was then held that 'Nature abhors a vacuum'—and, perhaps more plausibly, 'In nature there is an explanation for everything'—so it was contended that 'Nature abhors complexity.' Kant's Copernican Revolution shifted the responsibility for such desiderata from physical nature to the human intellect. Simplicity-tropism accordingly became not a feature of 'the real world', but rather one of 'the mechanisms of human thought' (though perhaps one that is hard-wired into the human intellect, as we would nowadays put it.) Kant acutely observed that what was at issue was a facet not of the teleology of *nature*, but of the teleology of *reason*, responsibility for which lay not with the theory but with the theorizers.

The subsequent Darwinian Revolution may be viewed as taking the process a step further. It removed the teleological element. Neither nature nor man's rational faculties were now seen as an ontological locus of simplicity-preference but its rationale was placed on a *strictly methodological* basis. And there is much justice in this position. For in the end responsibility for simplicity-tropism lies not with the hardware of human reason, but with its software—i.e. with the methodological principles that we ourselves employ because we find simpler theories easier to work with and more effective.

Hans Reichenbach has written: 'Actually in cases of inductive simplicity it is not economy which determines our choice.... We make the assumption that the simplest theory furnishes the best predictions. This assumption cannot be justified by convenience: it has a truth character and demands a justification within the theory of probability and induction.'[1] But this perspective is gravely misleading. What sort of consideration would possibly justify the supposition that 'the simplest theory furnishes the best predictions'? Any such belief is surely inappropriate. Induction with respect to the history of science itself—a constant series of errors of oversimplification—

---

[1] Hans Reichenbach, *Experience and Prediction* (Chicago: University of Chicago Press, 1938), 376. Compare: 'Imagine that a physicist...wants to draw a curve which passes through [points on a graph that represent] the data observed. It is well known that the physicist chooses the simplest curve; this is not to be regarded as a matter of convenience [for different] curves correspond as to the measurements observed, but they differ as to future measurements; hence they signify different predictions based on the same observational material. The choice of the simplest curve, consequently, depends on an inductive assumption: we believe that the simplest curve gives the best predictions.... If in such cases the question of simplicity plays a certain role for our decision, it is because we make the assumptions that the simplest theory furnishes the best predictions' (ibid. 375–6).

would soon undermine our confidence that nature operates in the way we would deem the simpler. On the contrary, the history of science is a highly repetitive story of simple theories giving way to more complicated and sophisticated ones. The Greeks had four elements; in the nineteenth century, Mendeleev had some eighty; we nowadays have a vast series of stability states. Aristotle's cosmos had only spheres; Ptolemy's added epicycles; ours has a virtually endless proliferation of complex orbits that only supercomputers can approximate. Greek science could be transmitted by a shelf of books; that of the Newtonian age required a roomful; ours requires vast storage structures filled not only with books and journals but with photographs, tapes, floppy disks, and so on. Of the quantities nowadays recognized as the fundamental constants of physics, only one was contemplated in Newton's physics, the universal gravitational constant.[2] It would be naïve—and quite wrong—to think that the course of scientific progress provides a world-picture of increasing simplicity. Just as organic evolution exfoliates ongoing diversity and complexity from a simple starting-point, so does cognitive evolution. The process at issue may be simple but is recursive, and involved working-out always engenders complexity. To claim the ontological simplicity of the real is somewhere between hyperbolic and absurd. Instead, our inductive practice insists upon the simplest issue-resolving answer—the simplest resolution that meets the conditions of the problem. And we take this line not because we know a priori that this simplest resolution will prove to be correct. (We know no such thing!) Rather, we adopt this answer—provisionally at least—just exactly because it is the least cumbersome and most economical way of providing a question resolution that does justice to the facts and demands of the situation. Reichenbach has thus turned things upside down here: it is indeed methodology that is at issue rather than any factual presumption or discovery to the effect that simpler theories provide better predictions.

The reality of it is that when other things are anything like equal, simpler theories are bound to be operationally more advantageous. We avoid needless complications whenever possible, because this is the course of an economy of effort. It is the general practice in scientific theory construction to give preference to

---

[2] See B. W. Petley, *The Fundamental Physical Constants and the Frontiers of Measurement* (Bristol: Hilger 1985).

- one-dimensional rather than multidimensional modes of description,
- quantitative rather than qualitative characterizations,
- lower- rather than higher-order polynomials,
- linear rather than non-linear differential equations.

The comparatively simpler is for this very reason easier to work with. In sum, we favour uniformity, analogy, simplicity, and the like exactly because they ease our cognitive labour. On such a perspective, simplicity is a factor that belongs to the practical order, pivoting on an operational economy that makes fewer demands upon our limited resources.

In the course of scientific inquiry, we seek for the most economical theory-accommodation for the amplest body of currently available experience. Induction—here short for 'the scientific method' in general—proceeds by way of constructing the most straightforward and economical structures able to house the available data comfortably while yet affording answers to our questions.[3]

This methodological commitment to rational economy does not prejudge or prejudice the substantively *ontological* issue of the complexity of nature. Natural science is emphatically *not* precommitted to a Principle of Simplicity in Nature, and this is fortunate, seeing that there really are no convincing grounds for supposing the 'simplicity' of the world's make-up. Instead, the so-called Principle of Simplicity is really a principle of complexity-management: 'Feel free to introduce complexity in your efforts to describe and explain nature's ways. But only when and where it is really needed. In so far as possible, keep it simple! Only introduce as much complexity as you really need for your scientific purposes of description, explanation, prediction, and control.' Simplicity-preference is based on the clearly method-oriented practical consideration that the simple hypotheses are the most convenient and advantageous for us to put to use in the context of our purposes. The Principle of Least Effort is in control here—the process is one of maximally economic means to the attainment of chosen ends. This amounts to a *theoretical* defence of inductive systematicity that in fact rests on *practical* considerations relating to the efficiencies of method. Accordingly, inductive systematicity is best approached with reference, not to reality as

---

[3] Details to fill in this telegraphic account are considered in the author's *Induction* (Oxford: Basil Blackwell, 1980).

such—or even merely our conception of it—but to the ways and means we employ in conceptualizing it.

To be sure, only time will eventually tell to what extent we can successfully move in the direction in which systematicity and its concomitant simplicity point. This is something that remains to be seen. (And here the importance of ultimate experiential retrovalidation comes in to supplement our commitment to methodological convenience.) But they clearly afford the most natural and promising starting-point. The systematically smoothest resolution of our questions is patently that which must be allowed to prevail—at any rate pro tem, until such time as its untenability becomes manifest. Where a simple solution will accommodate the data at hand, there is no good reason for turning elsewhere.

On such a perspective, then, our simplicity-based inductive practices are seen as a fundamentally regulative and procedural resource in the domain of inquiry, proceeding in implementation of the injunction: 'Do all you reasonably can to enhance the extent to which your cognitive commitments are simple and smoothly systematic.' It is, after all, a fundamental principle of rational procedure, operative just as much in the cognitive domain as anywhere else, that from among various alternatives that are anything like equally well qualified in other regards we should adopt the one that is the simplest, the most economical—in whatever modes of simplicity and economy are relevant.

1.3. Rationality and Economy

What matters for us finite beings is not ideal and certain knowledge in the light of complete and perfected information, but getting the best estimate that is actually obtainable here and now. We humans need to achieve both an intellectual and a physical accommodation to our environment. Now in regard to the former, rationality requires doing the best one can with the means at one's disposal, striving for the best results that one can expect to achieve within the range of one's resources, specifically including one's intellectual resources.

Accordingly, rationality has an ineliminable economic dimension since the effective use of limited resources is, after all, a crucial aspect of rationality. It is against reason to expend more resources on the realization of a given end than one needs to.[4] And it is against reason to expend more resources on the pursuit of a goal than it is worth—to do things in a more complex, inefficient, or ineffective way than is necessary in the circumstances. But it is also against reason to expend fewer resources in the pursuit of a goal than it is worth, unless these resources can be used to even better effect elsewhere. Cost-effectiveness—the proper co-ordination of costs and benefits in the pursuit of our ends—is an indispensable requisite of rationality.

This general situation obtains with particular force where the transaction of our specifically *cognitive* business is concerned. With any source of information or method of information acquisition, two salient questions arise:

1. *Utility*: How useful is it; how often and how pressingly do we have occasion/need to make use of it; how significant are the issues that rest on its availability; what sort of benefit does its possession engender?

2. *Cost*: How costly is its employment; how expensive (complicated, difficult, resource demanding) is its use?

A natural tendency is at work in human affairs—and indeed in the dealings of rational agents generally—to keep these two items in alignment so as to maintain a proper proportioning of costs and benefits. In particular:

1. If some instrumentality affords a comparatively inexpensive means to accomplishing a needed task, we incline to make more use of it.

2. If we need to achieve a certain end often, then we try to devise less expensive ways of achieving it.

Such principles of economic rationality not only explain why people use more staples than paper clips, but also account for important cognitive situations—for example, why the most frequently used words in a language tend to be among the shortest. (No ifs, ands, or buts about that!)

Economy of effort is a cardinal principle of rationality that helps to explain many aspects of the way in which we transact our cognitive business. Why are encyclopaedias organized alphabetically rather

---

[4] But is it indeed irrational to give a gift more costly than the social situation requires? By no means! It all depends on one's aims and ends, which may, on such an occasion, lie in a desire to cause the recipient surprise and pleasure, rather than merely doing the customary thing. There is an important difference between wastefulness and generosity.

than topically? Because this simplifies the search process. Why are accounts of people's doings or a nation's transactions standardly presented historically, with biographies and histories presented in chronological order? Because an account that moves from causes to effect simplifies understanding. Why do libraries group books together by topic and language rather than, say, alphabetically by author? Because this minimizes the difficulties of search and access. We are in a better position to understand innumerable features of the way in which people conduct their cognitive business once we take the economic aspect into account.

It is particularly noteworthy from such an economic point of view that there will be some conditions and circumstances in which the cost of question resolution—even assuming that it is possible in the prevailing state of the cognitive art—is simply too high relative to its value. There are (and are bound to be) circumstances in which the acquisition costs of information exceed the benefits or returns on its possession. In this regard, too, information is just like any other commodity. The price is sometimes more than we can afford and often greater than any conceivable benefit that would ensue. (This is why people generally do not count the number of hairs in their eyebrows.)

Rationality and economy are thus inextricably interconnected. Rational inquiry is a matter of epistemic optimizations, of achieving the best overall balance of cognitive benefits relative to cognitive costs. Cost-benefit calculation is the crux of the economy of effort at issue. The principle of least effort—construed in a duly intellectualized manner—is bound to be a salient feature of cognitive rationality.[5] A version of Occam's Razor obtains throughout the sphere of cognitive rationality: *complicationes non multiplicandae sund praeter necessitatem*. Efforts to secure and enlarge knowledge are worthwhile only in so far as they are cost-effective in that the resources we expend for these purposes are more than compensated for through benefits obtained—as is indeed very generally the case. But not always. We are, after all, finite beings who have only limited time and energy at our disposal. And even the development of knowledge, important though it is, is nevertheless of limited

---

[5] On this theme, see the important investigations of George K. Zipf, *Human Behavior and the Principle of Least Effort* (Cambridge, Mass.: Addison-Wesley Press, 1949). Zipf's investigations furnish a wide variety of interesting examples of how various of our cognitive proceedings exemplify a tendency to minimize the expenditure of energy.

value—it is not worth the expenditure of every minute of every day at our disposal.

The standard economic process of cost-effectiveness tropism is operative throughout the cognitive domain. Rational inquiry is rigorously subject to the economic impetus to securing maximal product for minimal expenditure. Concern for answering our questions in the most straightforward, most cost-effective way is a crucial aspect of cognitive rationality in its economic dimension.

The long and short of it is that the acquisition and management of information is a purposive human activity—like many or most of our endeavours. And as such it involves the ongoing expenditure of resources for the realization of the objectives—description, explanation, prediction, and control—that represent the defining characteristics of our cognitive endeavours. The balance of costs and benefits becomes critical here, and endows the cognitive enterprise with an unavoidably economic aspect.

1.4. The Regulative/Methodological Character of Cognitive Systematicity

It is important, however, to distinguish economy of means from economy of product—procedural from material economy. Simple tools or methods can, suitably used, create complicated results. A simple cognitive method, such as trial and error, can ultimately yield complex answers to difficult questions. Conversely, simple results are sometimes brought about in convoluted ways. A complicated method of inquiry or problem solving might yield easy and uncomplicated problem solutions. Our commitment to simplicity in scientific inquiry does not, in the end, prevent us from discovering whatever complexities are actually there. The role of the chances, chaos, and complexity *as an aspect of reality itself* cannot be precluded. Since the bearing of *cognitive* systematicity is regulative rather than descriptive in orientation it is altogether lacking in substantive and ontological involvements. For in the final analysis, it is not that nature avoids complexity, but that *we* do so—in so far as we find it possible.

Induction is no more than a search for cognitive order in the resolution of our questions, and our processes of inductive inquiry into nature are geared to reveal orderliness *if it is there*. When fishing, a net whose mesh has a certain area will catch fish of a certain size *if* any are present. Use of the net indicates a hope, perhaps even an expectation that the fish will be there, but certainly not a preassured foreknowledge of their presence. Nothing in the abstract logic of the situation guarantees a priori that we shall find order when we go looking for it in the world. (Our cognitive search for order and system may issue in a finding of disorder and chaos.) The question of whether the world is such that systematic knowledge of it is possible is an ultimately *contingent* question whose answer must itself emerge from our actual endeavours at systematization.

The parameters of cognitive systematicity—simplicity, regularity, coherence, conformity, and the rest—generally represent principles of economy of operation. They implement the idea of epistemic preferability or precedence, of presumption and burden of proof, by indicating where, in the absence of specific counterindications, our epistemic commitments are to be placed in weaving the fabric of our knowledge. In this way they are labour-saving devices for the avoidance of complications in the conduct of our cognitive business. Such a procedural/methodological mechanism does not prejudge or pre-empt any ultimate substantive finding, but it does decisively guide and control the process by which the answer—whatever it may be—is attained.

Accordingly, one need not prejudge that the world *is* a system to set about the enterprise of striving to know it systematically. The finding of ontological systematicity (orderliness, lawfulness) in nature—to whatever extent that nature indeed *is* systematic—is a substantive product of systematizing inquiry, rather than a needed input or presupposition for it. For it is a regulative or action-guiding *presumption* and not a constitutive or world-descriptive *principle* that is at issue—in the first instance at any rate.[6] We are to proceed as though nature in fact exhibited those modes of systematicity

---

[6] Charles Sanders Peirce took the sensible line that the principles such as those of the uniformity or systematicity of nature represent not so much a substantive *claim* as an action-guiding *insinuation*: 'Now you know how a malicious person who wishes to say something ill of another, prefers *insinuation*; that is, he speaks so vaguely that he suggests a great deal while he expressly says nothing at all. In this way he avoids being confronted by fact. It is the same with these principles of scientific inference. . . . They rather insinuate a uniformity than state it. And as insinuation always expresses the state of feeling of the person who uses it rather than anything concerning its object, so we may suppose these principles express rather the scientific attitude than a scientific result' (*Collected Papers* (Cambridge, Mass.: Harvard University Press, 1931–58), vii. sect. 7.134).

needed for systematizing inquiry to bear fruit. Its confirmation as in requisite degree present as a matter of descriptive fact at the *substantive* level is something that must come later on, in the course rather than at the outset of inquiry. The inductive method standard in rational inquiry thus emerges as a matter of the pursuit of systemic economy in the cognitive sphere.

Inductive simplicity and systematicity inhere in a regulative ideal of inquiry correlative with the procedural injunction: So organize your knowledge as to impart to it as much systematic structure as you possibly can! A cognitive venture based on the quest for simplicity and systematicity, while at first merely hopeful, is ultimately retro-validated in experience by the fact that its pursuit enables us to realize the fundamental aims and purposes of the cognitive enterprise more efficiently than the available alternatives. Initially, the pivotal issue is simply the matter of our convenience in doing what must be done to serve our purposes. The whole ontological question of the systematicity of nature can safely be left to await the results of the actual deployment of our inductive processes. No prior presuppositions are needed in that regard.

But does not the prospect that its objective may well be unattainable impede the appropriateness of adopting simplicity as an ideal of inquiry? Surely not. The validation of this cognitive ideal does *not* lie in the fact that its realization can be guaranteed a priori from the outset. We may in fact never realize it. But this possibility should never be allowed to impede our efforts to press the project of systematization as far as we possibly can. Here, as elsewhere, the validity of an ideal does not call for any prior guarantee of its ultimate realization. (What ideal is ever validated in that way?) To be sure, a hope of its eventual realization can never in principle be finally and totally demolished. But this feeble comfort is hardly sufficient to establish its propriety.

The long and short of it is that while we have no a priori assurance of ultimate success in the quest for systematicity, a standing presumption in favour of this key cognitive ideal is nevertheless rationally legitimate because of its furtherance of the inherent aims and objectives of the cognitive enterprise. In sum, the validation of systematicity as a cognitive ideal roots in the essentially practical consideration of its proven utility.

There is, however, another important aspect to the issue of the relation of the world's cognitive and ontological systematicity.

1.5. Cognitive Systematicity as an Indicator of Ontological Systematicity

Ontological systematicity relates to the orderliness and the lawfulness of nature—to its conformity to rules of various sorts. Now if nature were not rulish in exhibiting manifold regularities—if it were pervasively 'unruly' (say because its laws changed about rapidly and randomly)—then anything approaching a scientific study of the world would clearly be impossible. The modes of orderliness at issue in the various parameters of systematicity (simplicity, regularity, coherence, uniformity, consistency, and the rest) are all related to aspects of the workings of nature that underwrite the possibility of scientific inquiry.

If natural science is to be possible at all then our situation in nature must be such that our local environment is sufficiently systematic (orderly, regular) to permit the orderly conduct of rational inquiry, and thus, *a fortiori*, the existence of intelligent beings capable of it. If the world were not orderly (both in itself and as concerns the *modus operandi* of inquiring creatures), then there would be no uniformity in information-gathering, information-storage, etc., and consequently there would be no avenue to the acquisition of knowledge of the world—or indeed even putative knowledge of it. If the attainment—nay even the pursuit—of knowledge is to be possible for us, the world must be at any rate sufficiently orderly to permit of our cognitive functioning. This rulishness is basic to the very possibility of natural science. The aims of science—the description, explanation, prediction, and control of nature—would clearly be altogether unrealizable in a world that is badly asystematic. A significant degree of ontological systematicity *in* the world is (obviously) a causal requisite for realizing codificational systematicity in our knowledge *of* the world. Thus while the ontological systematicity of the world is not a conceptual presupposition for the success of systematizing inquiry, it is nevertheless—at least in some degree—a causal precondition for this success. A world that is insufficiently systematic and verges on chaos cannot provide an environment within which inductive learning is possible. (To be sure, a world that admits of knowledge-acquisition need not be a *total* system, partial systematicity will do—merely enough to permit orderly inquiry in our cosmic neighbourhood by beings constituted as we are.)

As these deliberations indicate, the rationale of our recourse to the parameters of inductive systematization is not *wholly* methodological but also has an ontological, realistic aspect, in that we learn by experience how to practice induction—that is, how to go about the process of a conservation of effort. Trial and error—that is, the course of experience—constrains us to bring methodological/procedural economy into alignment with substantive/ontological economy in our cognitive operations. In particular, the reification of the mechanisms of our simplest explanations (unobservable entities and the like) affords a powerful heuristic. It is the (empirically confirmed) efficacy of such a process that provides the ultimate justification for seeing science in *realistic* perspective. Thus we are well advised to accept unobservable entities not because their existence is somehow revealed in observation (which *ex hypothesi* it is not) but because experience shows that a methodology of inquiry predicated on such a simplifying assumption in the end affords our most efficient and effective resources.

The justification of relying on those systematicity-related virtues in the pursuit of our cognitive affairs will at first rest on an essentially instrumental basis. We incline initially to prefer the optimally systematic (simple, uniform) alternative, because this is the most economical, the most convenient, thing to do. But we persist in this course because experience shows the utilization of such economical methods to be efficient, to be optimally cost effective (relative to available alternative) for the realization of the task. For the pivotal fact is not that (as Reichenbach puts it) 'we make the assumption that the simplest theory furnishes the best predictions'—an assumption obviously ill-advised in the light of experience—but that plausible expectation preindicates and actual experience retrojustifies the supposition that a process of inquiry that proceeds on this basis is comparatively efficient in the realization of our cognitive goals. The crux is that we ultimately learn by *experience* (and thus through inductive reasoning itself) how to conduct our inductive business more effectively. Our recourse to induction—that is, *that* we proceed by its means—is justified instrumentally. For induction is a self-improving process. Experience can itself teach us that the guiding ideals of inductive practice (simplicity, conformity, generality, and the rest) can lead to improved performance in the transaction of our inductive business. By a cyclic feedback process of variation and trial, we learn to do induction more effectively. Economy, convenience, and efficiency play the crucial pioneering role in initially justifying our practice of inductive systematization on procedural and methodological grounds. But, in their turn, the issues of *effectiveness* and *success* come to predominate at the subsequent stage of retrospective revalidation *ex post facto*. And the question of the seemingly preestablished harmony co-ordinating these two theoretically disparate factors of convenience and effectiveness is ultimately resolved on the basis of evolutionary considerations in the order of rational selection.[7] For the *modus operandi* of a rational creature clearly makes for a selective pressure to use, retain, and transmit those processes that prove effective and efficient in the accomplishment of essential tasks.

And so, while our commitment to inductive systematicity is a matter of methodological convenience within the overall economy of rational procedure, nevertheless, it is in the final event not totally devoid of ontological commitments regarding the world's nature. To be sure, things need not *be* systematic to admit of systematic study and discussion: the systematicity of the real is not a prerequisite for systematicity in knowledge of it. (Knowledge need not share the features of its objects: to speak of a sober study of inebriation or a dispassionate analysis of passions is not a contradiction in terms.) However, while its converse fails, as we have seen, the implication

$$(X \text{ is ontologically systematic}) \rightarrow \left\{ \begin{array}{c} \text{information about } X \text{ is} \\ \text{in principle cognitively} \\ \text{systematizable} \end{array} \right\}$$

is nevertheless a necessary one. Ontological systematicity is in fact a sufficient condition for cognitive *systematizability*. For clearly such implications as the following will hold:

If no simple *account* of a thing is in principle realizable, then it cannot itself be simple, ontologically speaking.

If no coherent *explanation* of a process is in principle realizable, then it cannot itself be coherent, ontologically speaking.

If no uniform *description* of a thing is in principle realizable, then it cannot itself be uniform, ontologically speaking.

---

[7] Some other considerations relevant to these issues are canvassed in the author's *Methodological Pragmatism* (Oxford: Basil Blackwell, 1977) and *Cognitive Systematization* (Oxford: Basil Blackwell, 1979).

The parameters of systematicity are accordingly such that the basic principle holds:

> If a thing *is* itself ontologically simple (uniform, coherent, etc.), then a simple (uniform, coherent, etc.) *account* of it must in principle be possible (however difficult we may find its realization in practice).

Thus while cognitive systematicity cannot provide deductively necessitating evidence for ontological systematicity, nevertheless it certainly provides an *inductive* indication of ontological systematicity. And in fact, cognitive systematicity of a suitable kind affords the best—perhaps the only—empirical evidence we can ever actually obtain on behalf of ontological systematicity; the former constitutes the best available criterion or evidential indicator of the latter.

To be sure, the objection might well be made at this stage:

> Might there not be a theory which, in its make-up as a theory, is extremely complex, but according to which the *modus operandi* of nature itself is extremely simple?

But despite its surface plausibility this objection rests on a mistake. For nature cannot be simple (etc.) if our mental processes are not, seeing that we ourselves are a part of nature. If our intellectual dealings are not simple (or regular or—generally—systematic), then nature itself does not pervasively exhibit this characteristic either. The fact that our mental operations must be inserted into the world as a smoothly functioning integral part thereof means that a nature that incorporates such complex processes cannot be simple overall. (In theory it could be simple in everything that does not appertain to such processes but, as these processes are increasingly brought to bear upon nature itself, it becomes clear that the region of that which does not somehow appertain to them is continually diminished.) And if it turned out that we require a highly complex theory to account for the ways of human thought, then nature itself cannot be all that simple. And so in the end nature's cognitive systematicity provides an evidential indication—perhaps the best we actually have—of its ontological simplicity and/or systematicity.[8]

---

[8] Further relevant aspects of the matter are discussed in the author's *Cognitive Economy* (Pittsburgh: University of Pittsburgh Press, 1989), ch. 8.

2

The Complexity of Nature and the Cognitive Inexhaustibility of Things

SYNOPSIS

(1) A Law of Natural Complexity so operates as to render nature pervasively complex and inexhaustible in its details. (2) And this means that our characterization of the world's make-up and modus operandi can never be carried through to completion. (3) Our attempts at description can never exhaust the realm of natural fact. (4) Nor can we manage to arrive at a final and definitive account of the law structure of the world.

2.1. The Law of Natural Complexity

Much can be said for the dictum that truth is stranger than fiction. And the reason for this is straightforward. Nature is vastly more complex than the human brain—if only because we ourselves are merely a minor constituent of nature itself. Moreover, the human intellect's capacity for complexity management is limited and the states of affairs that our minds can envision are vastly fewer and simpler than those that nature can present. As best we can tell from our own experience of it, nature's intricacy proceeds without stop.

The impenetrable and unchanging atoms of the ancient Greeks have become increasingly dematerialized and ethereal, composed of automatically smaller processes. As we increase the power of our particle accelerators, our view of the make-up of the subatomic realm becomes not only ever different but also ever stranger. The history of science is the story of an ever-increasing complexity in our account of things. (The volume of our information about the housefly is greater than Aristotle's about the whole of the animal kingdom.) And we cannot even begin to conceive the facts and phenomena that will figure on the agenda of the science of the future. Its complexity is one of the most striking and characteristic features of reality in general—and indeed of anything in particular that is real. As G. W. Leibniz stressed as early as the seventeenth-century, real existence is always involved in an unending elaborateness of *detail*.[1] Anything that exists in this world exhibits an infinite descriptive depth. No account of it can come to the end of the line. None can ever manage to tell us everything that there is to know about something real—none can say all that there is to be said. Nature's detail is inexhaustible.

It is important for the world's functioning—and for our understanding of it—that the details often do not matter to the particular issue on the agenda, that fine-grained differences produce no large consequences here. What an individual decides to do—whether to buy that umbrella or not—makes no difference to the American economy: its money supply, inflation rate, balance of trade, etc., will all remain unaffected. But not every sort of system is like that. Natural systems can be classified into two types: the linear and the non-linear.[2] Linear systems admit of approximation. If we oversimplify them we change nothing essential: the results we obtain by working with the simplified models will approximate the condition of their more complex counterparts in the real world. Small-scale departures from reality make no significant difference. But non-linear systems behave differently. Here small variations—even undetectably small ones—can make for great differences. Accordingly, simplification—let alone oversimplification—can prove fatal: even the smallest miss can prove to be as good as a mile as far as outcomes are concerned. Differentiating between an essential core and a negligible periphery is beyond implementation here. Every detail matters—none is 'irrelevant' or 'negligible'. Simplified models will accordingly be of no help at all—with non-linearity it is a matter of all or nothing.

And so, perhaps the most fundamental question that can be asked of any natural system is: Is it linear or non-linear? Everything turns on this, since non-linear systems must be studied holistically and comprehensively. And a system whose formative subsystems are to any

---

[1] G. W. Leibniz, *Monadology*, sect. 37.
[2] The 'linearity' at issue here is that of physics, which so characterizes a system whose functioning can be described by the smooth curves of everywhere differentiable equations. The behaviour of such systems is thus calculation-friendly and predictable.

appreciable extent non-linear thereby becomes immensely complex. Just here lies the reason why intricately convoluted complex systems such as biological evolution or human history or electoral politics—processes where seemingly haphazard and 'external' events can continually effect outcomes—are so complex that the questions they pose for us defy calculation and foreclose the prospect of computational problem-solving. The machinations of a deranged assassin can make an enormous difference for the entire nation whose leader is his victim. Non-linear systems are always far less tractable, be it operationally or cognitively. And for reasons deeply rooted in its *modus operandi*, nature is non-linear to an extent greater than we like to think.

As already indicated, we do well from a methodological point of view to struggle against such complexity, inclining to the assumption that the systems we confront are cognitively tractable—that we can (over)simplify and get away with it. Methodological Simplificationism—the presumption of simplicity—is an important, common, and legitimate instrument of inquiry. But it has to be acknowledged as being no more than that—a mere *presumption*. And we recognize full well that the realities of a difficult world will often fail to accommodate us in this regard: often—though fortunately not predominantly, let alone always. For intelligence could not emerge and make its evolutionary way in a world where it could get no purchase and its efforts proved constantly abortive.

C. S. Peirce never tired of emphasizing nature's inherent tendency to complexity proliferation. He wrote:

Evolution means nothing but *growth* in the widest sense of that word. Reproduction, of course, is merely one of the incidents of growth. And what is growth? Not mere increase. Spencer says it is the passage from the homogeneous to the heterogeneous—or, if we prefer English to Spencerese—*diversification*. That is certainly an important factor of it. Spencer further says that it is a passage from the unorganized to the organized; but that part of the definition is so obscure that I will leave it aside for the present. But think what an astonishing idea this of *diversification* is! Is there such a thing in nature as increase of variety? Were things simpler, was variety less in the original nebula from which the solar system is supposed to have grown than it is now when the land and the sea swarm with animal and vegetable forms with their intricate anatomies and still more wonderful economies? It would seem as if there were an increase in variety, would it not?[3]

[3] Charles S. Peirce, *Collected Papers* (Cambridge, Mass.: Harvard University Press, 1931), i. sect. 1.174.

The tenor of these observations is just. The fact is that complexity is self-potentiating. Complex systems generally engender further principles of order that produce yet greater complexities. Complex organisms create an impetus towards complex societies, complex machines towards complex industries, complex armaments towards complex armies. And the world's complexity means that there is, now and always, more to reality than our science—or for that matter our speculation and our philosophy—is able to dream of.

2.2. Hidden Depths

The quest for knowledge embarks us on an infinite journey. From finitely many axioms, reason can generate a potential infinity of theorems; from finitely many words, thought can exfoliate a potential infinity of sentences; from finitely many data, reflection can extract a potential infinity of items of information. Even with respect to a world of finitely many objects, the process of reflecting upon these objects can, in principle, go on unendingly. One can enquire about their features, the features of these features, and so on. Or again, one can consider their relations, the relations among those relations, and so on. Thought—abstraction, reflection, analysis—is an inherently ampliative process. As in physical reflection mirror images can reflect one another indefinitely, so mental reflection can go on and on. Given a start, however modest, thought can advance into ever new conceptual domains. The circumstance of its starting out from a finite basis does *not* mean that it need ever run out of impetus (as the example of Shakespearean scholarship seems to illustrate).

The number of true descriptive remarks that can be made about a real thing—about any actual item of the world's actual furnishings—is theoretically inexhaustible. For example, take a stone. Consider its physical features: its shape, its surface texture, its chemistry, etc. And then consider its causal background: its subsequent genesis and history. Then consider its functional aspects as relevant to its uses by the stonemason, or the architect, or the landscape decorator, etc. There is, in principle, no theoretical limit to the different lines of consideration available to yield descriptive truths about a thing, so that the totality of potentially available facts about a thing—about anything real whatever—is in principle inexhaustible.

In particular, the world's descriptive complexity is literally limit-less. Ever since the days of Locke and Leibniz in the seventeenth century, theorists have endorsed the conception that new ideas can always be amplified by recombinations of the old. And once this sort of process gets under way, there is no reason of principle why it should ever have to come to a stop. Evolving science can always embed things in new modes of lawful order.

Reality/existence is not homogeneous. It embraces distinct realms. There is the physicist's world of material existence, the symbolic realm of language and mathematics, the conceptual realm of ideas and propositions, the artefactual realm of literature, drama, music, and so on. And all of these are capable of further subdivision, even as the material realm of substantial objects can be divided along various lines of consideration: physical, biological, social, etc. John Maynard Key-nes's Principle of Limited Variety is simply wrong: there is no inherent limit to the number of distinct kinds or categories to which the things of this world can belong. In the study of natural phenomena further distinctions are always possible and our distinctions will always admit in principle of additional sophistication and complication. As best as we can possibly tell, natural reality has an infinite descriptive depth. It confronts us with a Law of Natural Complexity: *There is no limit to the number of natural kinds to which any concrete particular belongs.*

And even where these realms overlap in their contents (as music can be represented in scores, dramas in staged performances, geometric forms in printed formulas and diagrams, etc.—all of which are physical representations of very different sorts of things) nevertheless these realms are conceptually separate. As even a cursory survey of typographical scripts shows, no particular physical shape or shapes can ever entirely capture a letter of the alphabet.

Every realm of being has its own distinctive family of conceptual categories, and none of these can be reduced or translated into the others. We can establish *correspondences* between the states of one realm and that of others (can digitalize music or represent numbers on an abacus). But such correspondences never manage to transpose meanings from one domain to the other. To take the deliberations of one realm as literal reiterations of another is always to commit a category mistake—a conflation or confusion of inherently different sorts of things.

It is helpful to introduce a distinction at this stage. On the standard conception of the matter, a 'truth' is something to be understood in *linguistic* terms—the representation of a fact through its statement in some actual language. Any correct statement in some actual language formulates a truth. (And the converse obtains as well: a truth must be encapsulated in a statement, and cannot exist without linguistic embodiment.) A 'fact', on the other hand, is not a linguistic entity at all, but an actual circumstance or state of affairs—a condition of things existing in the world. Anything that is correctly characterizable in some *possible* language constitutes a fact.[4]

Every truth must state a fact, but it is not only possible but indeed to be expected that there will be facts that cannot be stated in any actually available language—and which thus fail to be captured as truths. Facts afford *potential* truths whose actualization as such hinges on the availability of appropriate linguistic machinery for their formulation. Truths involve a one-parameter probability range: they include whatever can be correctly stated in some (actual) language. But facts involve a two-parameter probability range comprising whatever *can* be stated truly in some *possible* language. Truths are *actualistically* language-correlative, while facts are *possibilistically* language-correlative statable in principle, though very possibly not in fact.[5]

Accordingly, it must be presumed that there are facts that we cannot manage to formulate as truths, though it will obviously be impossible to give concrete examples of this phenomenon—any more than one can implement the idea of the incompleteness of one's knowledge by citing an example of a truth that one does not accept as such.[6]

[4] Our position can come to terms with P. F. Strawson's precept that 'facts are what statements (when true) state'. ('Truth', *Proceedings of the Aristotelian Society*, Suppl. 24 (1950), 129–56; see p. 136.) Difficulty would ensue only if an 'only' were inserted.

[5] But can any sense be made of the idea of *merely* possible (i.e. possible but non-actual) languages? Of course it can! Once we have a generalized conception (or definition) of a certain kind of thing—be it a language or a caterpillar—then we are inevitably in a position to suppose the prospect of things meeting these conditions are over and above those that in fact do so. The prospect of mooting certain 'mere' possibilities cannot be denied—that, after all, is just what possibilities are all about.

[6] Note, however, that if a Davidsonian translation argument to the effect that 'if it's sayable at all, then, it's sayable in *our* language' were to succeed—which it does not—then the matter would stand on a different footing. For it would then follow that any possible language can state no more than what can be stated in our own (actual) language. And then the realm of facts (i.e. what is (correctly) statable in some *possible* language) and that of truths (i.e. what is (correctly) statable in some *actual* language) would necessarily coincide. Accordingly, our thesis that the range of facts is larger than that of truths hinges crucially upon a failure of such a translation argument. And, of course, fail it does. (See Donald Davidson, 'The Very Idea of a Conceptual Scheme', *Proceedings and Addresses of the American Philosophical Association*, 47 (1973–4) 5–20, and also the critique of his position in the author's *Empirical Inquiry* (Totowa, NJ: Rowman Littlefield, 1982), ch. 2.)

After all, in real life, languages are never full-formed and a conceptual basis is never 'fixed and given'. Any adequate theory of inquiry must recognize that the ongoing process of information acquisition at issue in science is a process of *conceptual* innovation, which always leaves certain facts about things wholly outside the cognitive range of the inquirers of any particular period. Even with such familiar things as birds, trees, and clouds, we are involved in a constant reconceptualization in the course of progress in genetics, evolutionary theory, and hydro-dynamics. Any adequate world-view must recognize that the ongoing progress of scientific inquiry is a process of *conceptual* innovation that always leaves various facts about the things of this world wholly outside the cognitive range of the inquirers of any particular period. Now there will always be more facts about any real thing than we can ever manage to capture through the truths that we can formulate about it. One reason for this is the fundamentally progressive nature of knowledge in a world domain of potentially ongoing discovery. But another, deeper reason, lies in the circumstance that any *n* facts give rise to *n*! factual combinations that themselves represent further facts. The domain of fact inevitably transcends the limits of our capacity to express it, and *a fortiori* those of our capacity to canvass it in overt detail. There are always bound to be more facts than we are able to capture in our linguistic terminology. There is always more to be said than the propositions of any particular set—or indeed of any particular language—enable us to say.[7]

At this point, the following objection may well arise:

One single suitably general truth can encapsulate infinitely many descriptive facts—even a transdenumerable infinity of them. For example, in saying of a particular spring that it obeys Hooke's law (over a certain range)—assigning it the infinitely rich disposition to displace proportionally with imposed weights—I have implicitly provided for a transdenumerable infinity of descriptive consequences by means of the continuous parameter at issue. Accordingly, while it is true that the actual deductions which one can carry out from an axiomatic basis are denumerable, they can certainly manage to 'cover'—at a certain level of implicitness—a transdenumerable range of descriptive fact.

But of course the process envisioned here allows for only one very limited sort of infinitism: the positing of a particular value within

<hr>

[7] See Patrick Grim, *The Incomplete Universe: Totality, Knowledge, and Truth* (Cambridge, Mass.: MIT Press, 1991).

one and the same infinitistic range of determination—the fixing of a special case within a prespecified spectrum. The objection is thus transcended when one recalls the Law of Natural Complexity's contention that there is in principle no theoretical limit to the lines of consideration available to provide descriptive perspectives upon a thing—that the range of descriptive spectra can always, in principle, be extended. The limitless descriptive complexity of the world's concrete things establishes the need for acknowledging a clear contrast between the manifold of the *discerned* properties of things as we have established them to date (always a finite collection) and their *actual* properties (which are potentially limitless).

To be sure, the limitlessness of the world's descriptive complexity does not mean that we cannot say how things stand by way of a reasonable approximation. We can always oversimplify matters—for example by specifying how things normally and usually comport themselves within the range of our observation. And often this is good enough for our practical and even our cognitive purposes. But, of course, it is an inevitable fact of life that the *actual* course of events is not always and everywhere normality-conforming: in the real world matters all too often eventuate in ways that depart from what we see as the usual course. Those oversimplifications of ours are no more than useful rules of thumb. It is exactly because reality is too complicated to be captured by our facile generalizations—is too full of vagaries and quirks—that we must constantly resort to qualifying locutions such as 'generally', 'standardly', and the like.[8] If we insisted on 'telling it exactly as it is', then we could not get there from here. However adequately they may function at the local level of their characteristic applications, seen as a whole our 'models of reality' are no more than rough approximations.[9]

2.3. Descriptive Incompleteness

Neither can we (truthfully and correctly) characterize nature exactly, nor can we manage to do so completely. We have to proceed by processual approximations. And this means that there is a need for

---

[8] Compare the author's *Philosophical Standardism* (Pittsburgh: University of Pittsburgh Press, 1994).

[9] On these issues see Nancy Cartwright, *How the Laws of Physics Lie* (Oxford: Clarendon Press, 1983).

different disciplines in the study of a complex world. All epistemo-
logy is local (as all politics is said to be): our proper *modus operandi*
in matters of inquiry must always be attuned to the local conditions
that prevail in the particular public area at issue. There is no single,
unique way of organizing our interests here—questions and particulars about nature. The physicists, the chemists, the biologists, the
economists, none have a monopoly on the study of the real. The
prospect of proliferating disciplines is inherent in that of a multi-
plication of the perspectives of consideration we ourselves bring to
nature's cognitive domestication.[10]

Our description of anything in nature is never exhaustive: they
always admit of further elaborative detail. Its inner structure and
external relationships can always be characterized more fully. There is
always more to be said. Everything in the world—no matter how
large or small—has involvements and ramifications about which
more remains to be said.

To be sure, we may always lose interest after a while. Our interest is
always governed by some aspect of our own concerns and principles.
And in due course further information becomes irrelevant to these.
(When we know that someone at large in the room is a homicidal
maniac, the issue of his cholesterol level may well become irrelevant
for us.) But this issue of diminishing returns is one that relates to our
own purposes and concerns. It does not countervail against the fact
that the truth of the matter is always open to further elaboration.
Whatever the topic of consideration may be, our knowledge of any
given matter of fact will never be complete. The real has an inner
complexity that is humanly inexhaustible and the range of fact
inevitably outruns that of articulable truth.

The upshot is clear. *The descriptions that we can ever actually
provide for real particulars are never complete.* The detail of the real
is bound to outrun our descriptive accomplishments: the domain of
thing-characterizing fact inevitably transcends the limits of our capacity to express it, and *a fortiori* those of our capacity to canvass
completely. We have every reason to presume reality to be cognitively
inexhaustible. In the description of concrete particulars we are
caught up in an inexhaustible detail: there are always bound to be
more descriptive facts about things than we are able to capture

---

[10] On this theme see John Dupré, *The Disorder of Things* (Cambridge, Mass.: Harvard
University Press, 1993).

explicitly with our linguistic machinery. A precommitment to description-transcending features—no matter how far description is actually pushed—is essential to our conception of what it is to be a real, concrete object.

2.4. Cognitive Incompleteness

This cognitive opacity of real things means that we are not—and will never be—in a position to avoid the contrast between things as we think them to be and things as they actually and truly are. Their susceptibility to further elaborate detail—and to changes of mind regarding this further detail—is built into our very conception of a 'real thing'. And the situation is much the same when our concern is not with physical things, but with *types* of such things. To say that something is copper or magnetic is to claim a good deal more than that it has the properties we think copper or magnetic things have, and to say more than that it meets our test conditions for being copper (or being magnetic). It is to say that this thing *is* copper or magnetic. And this is an issue regarding which we are prepared at least to contemplate the prospect that we have got it wrong.

It is worthwhile to examine more closely the considerations that indicate the inherent incompleteness of our knowledge of things.[11]

To begin with, it is clear that, as we standardly think about things within the conceptual framework of our fact-oriented thought and discourse, *any* real physical object has more facets than it will ever actually manifest in experience. For every objective property of a real thing has consequences of a dispositional character and these are never surveyable *in toto* because the dispositions that particular concrete things inevitably have endow them with an infinitistic aspect that cannot be comprehended within experience.[12] This

---

[11] On this theme see also Vincent Julian Fecher, *Error, Deception, and Incomplete Truth* (Rome: Officium Libri Catholici, 1975).

[12] To be sure, *abstract* things, such as colours or numbers, will not have dispositional properties. For being divisible by 4 is not a *disposition* of 16. Plato got the matter right in Book VII of the *Republic*. In the realm of *abstracta*, such as those of mathematics, there are not genuine *processes*—and process is a requisite of dispositions. Of course, there may be dispositional truths in which numbers (or colours, etc.) figure that do not issue in any dispositional properties of these numbers (or colours, etc.) themselves—a truth, for example, such as my predilection for odd numbers. But if a truth (or supposed truth) does no more than to convey how someone *thinks* about a thing, then it does not indicate any property of the thing itself. In any case, however, the subsequent discussion will focus

desk, for example, has a limitless manifold of phenomenal features of the type: 'having a certain appearance from a particular point of view'. It is perfectly clear that most of these will never be actualized in experience. Moreover, a thing *is* what it *does*: entity and lawfulness are co-ordinated correlates—a good Kantian point. And this fact that things demand lawful comportment means that the finitude of experience precludes any prospect of the *exhaustive* manifestation of the descriptive facets of any real things.[13]

Moreover, physical things not only have more properties than they ever *will* overtly manifest, but they have more than they possibly ever *can* manifest. This is so because the dispositional properties of things always involve what might be characterized as *mutually pre-emptive* conditions of realization. A cube of sugar, for example, has the dispositional property of reacting in a particular way if subjected to a temperature of 10,000 °C and of reacting in a certain way if placed for 100 hours in a large, turbulent body of water. But if either of these conditions is ever realized, it will destroy the lump of sugar as a lump of sugar, and thus block the prospect of its ever bringing the other property to manifestation. The perfectly possible realization of various dispositions may fail to be mutually *compossible*, and so the dispositional properties of a thing cannot ever be manifested completely—not just in practice, but in principle. Our objective claims about real things always commit us to more than we can actually ever determine about them.

The existence of this latent sector is a crucial feature of our conception of a real thing. Neither in fact nor in thought can we ever simply put it away. To say of the apple that its only features are those it actually manifests is to run afoul of our conception of an apple. To deny—or even merely to refuse to be committed to the claim—that it *would* manifest particular features *if* certain conditions came about (for example, that it would have such-and-such a taste if eaten) is to be driven to withdrawing the claim that it is an apple. The process of corroborating the implicit contents of our objective factual claims about something real is potentially endless, and such

on *realia* in contrast to *fictionalia* and *concreta* in contrast to *abstracta*. (Fictional things, however, *can* have dispositions: Sherlock Holmes was addicted to cocaine, for example. Their difference from *realia* is dealt with below.)

[13] This aspect of objectivity was justly stressed in the 'Second Analogy' of Kant's *Critique of Pure Reason*, though his discussion rests on ideas already contemplated by Leibniz, *Philosophische Schriften*, ed. C. I. Gerhardt (Berlin: Weidmann, 1890), vii. 319–22.

judgments are thus 'non-terminating' in C. I. Lewis's sense.[14] This cognitive depth of our objective factual claims inherent in the fact that their *content* will always outrun the evidence for making them means that the endorsement of any such claim always involves some element of evidence-transcending conjecture.

The concepts at issue (namely experience and manifestation) are such that we can only ever *experience* those features of a real thing that it actually *manifests*. But the preceding considerations show that real things always have more experientially manifestable properties than they can ever actually manifest in experience. The experienced portion of a thing is similar to the part of the iceberg that shows above water. All real things are necessarily thought of as having hidden depths that extend beyond the limits, not only of experience, but also of experientiability. To say of something that it is an apple or a stone or a tree is to become committed to claims about it that go beyond the data we have—and even beyond those which we can, in the nature of things, ever actually acquire. The 'meaning' inherent in the assertoric commitments of our factual statements is never exhausted by its verification. Real things are cognitively opaque—we cannot see to the bottom of them. Our knowledge of such things can thus become more *extensive* without thereby becoming more *complete*, since definite completeness is an unrealistic idea in a context where new dimensions of significance can open up.

In this regard, however, real things differ in an interesting and important way from their fictional cousins. To make this difference plain, it is useful to distinguish between two types of information about a thing, namely that which is *generic* and that which is not. Generic information relates to those features of a thing which it has in common with everything else of its kind or type. For example, a particular snowflake will share with all others certain facts about its structure, its hexagonal form, its chemical composition, its melting point, etc. On the other hand, it will also have various properties which it does not share with other members of its own 'lowest species' in the classificatory order—its particular shape, for example, or the angular momentum of its descent. These are its non-generic features.

---

[14] See C. I. Lewis, *An Analysis of Knowledge and Valuation* (La Salle, Ill.: Open Court, 1962), 180–1.

Now a key about *fictional* particulars is that they are of finite cognitive depth. In discoursing about them we shall ultimately run out of steam as regards their non-generic features. A point will always be reached when one cannot say anything further that is characteristically new about them—presenting non-generic information that is not inferentially implicit in what has already been said.[15] New generic information can, of course, always be forthcoming through the progress of science. When we learn more about coal-in-general then we know more about the coal in Sherlock Holmes's grate. But the finitude of their cognitive depth means that the presentation of ampliatively novel non-generic information must by the very nature of the case come to a stop when fictional things are at issue.

With *real* things, on the other hand, there is no reason of principle why the provision of non-generically idiosyncratic information need ever be terminated. On the contrary, we have every reason to presume these things to be cognitively inexhaustible. A precommitment to description-transcending features—no matter how far description is pushed—is essential to our conception of a real thing. Something whose character is exhaustible by linguistic characterization would thereby be marked as fictional rather than real.[16]

2.5. The Dynamic Aspect of Descriptive Inexhaustibility: the Instability of Knowledge

Nor is this the end of the story. The preceding considerations regarding the descriptive complexity of things relate to the limits of knowledge that can be rationalized on *a fixed and given* conceptual basis—a fully formed and developed language. But in real life languages are never fully formed and a conceptual basis is never fixed and given. The prospect of change can never be eliminated in this cognitive domain since the properties of anything real are literally open-ended so that we can always discover more of them. Even if we were (surely

---

[15] To deny inferentially implicit information the title of 'novelty', is not, of course, to say that it cannot surprise us in view of the limitations of our own deductive powers.

[16] This also explains why the dispute over mathematical realism (Platonism) has little bearing on the issue of physical realism. Mathematical entities are akin to fictional entities in this—that we can only say about them what we can extract by deductive means from what we have explicitly put into their defining characterization. These abstract entities do not have non-generic properties since each is a 'lowest species' unto itself.

mistakenly) to view the world's descriptive nature as inherently finitistic—espousing that mistaken Keynesian Principle of Limited Variety to the effect that nature can be portrayed descriptively with the materials of a finite taxonomic scheme—we can never rest assured that the progress of science will not lead to an indefinite series of changes of mind regarding this finite register of descriptive materials. This conforms exactly to our expectation in these matters. Be the items in question elm trees, volcanoes, or quarks, we have every expectation that in the course of future scientific progress people will come to view their origins and their properties differently from the way we do at this juncture. For the fact of it is that where the real things of the world are concerned, we not only expect to learn more about them in the course of scientific inquiry, we expect to have to change our minds about their nature and modes of comportment. And when the conceptions at issue are different so are the claims that we make by their measures.

Any adequate theory of inquiry must recognize that the ongoing process of information enhancement in scientific inquiry is a process of *conceptual* innovation that always leaves certain facts about things wholly outside the cognitive range of the inquirers of any particular period. Caesar did not know—and in the then existing state of the cognitive art could not have known—that his sword contained tungsten and carbon. There will always be facts about a thing that we do not *know* because we cannot even *conceive* of them within the prevailing conceptual order of things. To grasp such a fact would call for taking a perspective of consideration that as yet we simply do not have, since the state of knowledge (or purported knowledge) has not and indeed cannot yet reach a point at which such a consideration is feasible.

The language of emergence can perhaps be deployed usefully to make the point. But here emergence is not one of the features of things, but one of our unfolding information about them. Blood circulated in the human body well before Harvey; substances containing uranium were radioactive before Becquerel. The emergence at issue relates to our cognitive mechanisms of conceptualization, not to the *objects* of our consideration in and of themselves. Real-world objects must be conceived of realistically, as antecedent to any cognitive encounter, as being there right along—'pregiven' as Edmund Husserl put it. Those cognitive changes or innovations are to be conceptualized as something that occurs on *our* side of the cognitive transaction, rather than on the side of the *objects* with which we deal.

To be a real thing is to be something regarding which we can always, in principle, acquire further new information—information that may not only supplement but even correct that which has previously been acquired. This view of the situation is supported rather than impeded once we abandon the naïve cumulativist/preservationist view of knowledge acquisition for the view that new discoveries need not *augment* but can *displace* old ones. With further inquiry, we may come to recognize the error of our earlier ways of thinking about the things at issue. We realize that people will come to think differently about things from the way we do—even when thoroughly familiar things are at issue—recognizing that scientific progress generally entails fundamental changes of mind about how things work in the world. And this recognition of incomplete information is inherent in the very nature of our conception of a 'real thing'. It is a crucial facet of our epistemic stance towards the real world to recognize that every part and parcel of it has features lying beyond our present cognitive reach—at *any* 'present' whatsoever.

It is, of course, imaginable that natural science will come to a stop, not in the trivial sense of a cessation of intelligent life, but rather in Charles Sanders Peirce's more interesting sense of eventually reaching a condition after which even indefinitely ongoing effort at inquiry will not—and indeed actually *cannot*—produce any significant change. Such a position is, in theory, possible. But we can never *know*—be it in practice or in principle—that it is actually realized. We can never establish that science has attained such an omega-condition of final completion: the possibility of further change lying 'just around the corner' can never be ruled out finally and decisively. We thus have no alternative but to *presume* that our science is still imperfect and incomplete, that no matter how far we have pushed our inquiries in any direction, regions of *terra incognita* yet lie beyond. And this means that to be realistic we must take the stance that our conception of real things, no matter how elaborately developed, will always be provisional and corrigible. Reality has hidden reserves; it is deeper than our knowledge of it. As the history of science amply indicates, the impact of later, fuller knowledge, almost invariably shows that matters are in fact far more complex than one thinks them to be.

2.6. The Complexification of Science

As these considerations indicate, the developmental tendency of natural science is generally in the direction of greater complication and sophistication. Herbert Spencer argued long ago that evolution is characterized by von Baer's law of development 'from the homogeneous to the heterogeneous' and thereby produces an ever-increasing definition of detail and complexity of articulation.[17] As Spencer saw it, organic species in the course of their development need to overcome a successive series of environmental obstacles to their survival and with each successful turning along the maze of developmental challenges the organism becomes selectively more highly specialized in its bio-design, and thereby more tightly attuned to the particular features of its ecological context.[18] Now this view of the developmental process may or may not be correct for *biological* evolution, but there can be little question about its holding for *cognitive* evolution. Evolution, be it natural or rational—whether of animal species or of literary genres—progressively confronts us with products of greater and greater complexity.[19]

In consequence, our cognitive efforts manifest a Manichaean-style struggle between complexity and simplicity—between the impetus to comprehensiveness (amplitude) and the impetus to system (economy). We want our theories to be as extensive and all-encompassing as possible and at the same time to be elegant and economical. The first desideratum pulls in one direction, the second in the other. And the accommodation reached here is never actually stable. As our experience expands in the quest for greater adequacy and comprehensiveness, the old theory structures become destabilized—the old theories no longer fit the full range of available fact. And so the theoretician goes back to the old drawing board. What he comes up with here is—and in the circumstances almost invariably will be—something more elaborate, more *complex* than what was able to do

---

[17] Herbert Spencer, *First Principles*, 7th edn. (London: Methuen, 1889); see Pt. II, 'The Law of Evolution', sects. 14–17.

[18] On the process in general see John H. Holland, *Hidden Order: How Adaptation Builds Complexity* (Reading, Mass.: Addison-Wesley, 1995). Regarding the specifically evolutionary aspect of the process see Robert N. Brandon, *Adaptation and Environment* (Princeton: Princeton University Press, 1990).

[19] On the issues of this paragraph compare Stuart Kaufmann, *At Home in the Universe: The Search for the Laws of Self-Organization and Complexity* (New York: Oxford University Press, 1995).

the job before those new complications arose (though we do, of course, sometimes achieve local simplifications within an overall global complexification).

It is worthwhile to examine somewhat more closely the ramifications of complexity in the domain of cognition, now focusing upon science in particular. Progress in natural science is a process of dialogue or debate in a reciprocal interaction between theoreticians and experimentalists. The experimentalists probe nature to discern its reactions, to seek out phenomena. And the theoreticians take the resultant data and weave about them a fabric of hypotheses that is able to resolve our questions. Seeking to devise a framework of rational understanding, they construct their explanatory models to accommodate the findings that the experimentalists put at their disposal. Thereafter, once the theoreticians have had their say, the ball returns to the experimentalists' court. Employing new, more powerful means for probing nature, they bring new phenomena to view, new data for accommodation. Precisely because these data are new and inherently unpredictable on the basis of earlier knowledge, they often fail to fit the old theories. Theory extrapolations from the old data could not encompass them; the old theories do not accommodate them. A disequilibrium thus arises between available theory and novel data, and at this stage, the ball re-enters the theoreticians' court. New theories must be devised to accommodate the new, nonconforming data. Accordingly, the theoreticians set about building a new theoretical structure to accommodate the new data. They endeavour to restore the equilibrium between theory and data once more. And when they succeed, the ball returns to the experimentalists' court, and the whole process starts over again.

Scientific theory-formation is, in general, a matter of spotting a local regularity of phenomena in parametric space and then projecting it across the board, maintaining it globally. But the theoretical claims of science are themselves never small-scale and local—they are not spatiotemporally localized and they are not parametrically localized either. They stipulate—most ambitiously—how things are always and everywhere. But with the enhancement of investigative technology, the window through which we can look out upon nature's parametric space becomes constantly enlarged. In developing natural science we use this window of capability to scrutinize parametric space, continually augmenting our data-base and then generalizing upon what we see. What we have here is not a lunar landscape where once we have seen one sector we have seen it all, and where theory-projections from lesser data generally remain in place when further data comes our way. Instead it does not require a sophisticated knowledge of history of science to realize that our worst fears are usually realized—that our theories seldom if ever survive intact in the wake of substantial extensions in our cognitive access to new sectors of nature's parametric space. The history of science is a sequence of episodes of leaping to the wrong conclusions because new observational findings indicate matters are not quite so simple as heretofore thought. As ample experience indicates, our ideas about nature are subject to constant and often radical change-demanding stresses as we explore parametric space more extensively. The technologically mediated entry into new regions of parameter space constantly destabilizes the attained equilibrium between data and theory. Physical nature invariably exhibits a very different aspect when viewed from the vantage point of different levels of sophistication in the technology of nature–investigator interaction.[20] The possibility of change is ever-present. The ongoing destabilization of scientific theories is the price we pay for operating a simplicity-geared cognitive methodology in an actually complex world.

Consider the books and documents that outfit our libraries. At the base level there are topical materials, novels, say, or mathematical treatises, or biographical works. At the next level of aggregation we have such things as collective plot summaries, comparative critical studies, synthetic monographs, and collective author biographies. This in turn leads to the next level of reference works: bibliographies, encyclopaedias, topical dictionaries, citation studies, and the like. And then there remains the yet higher level of catalogues, document indices, and so on. Such a hierarchical structuring betokens our unavoidable but also unwinnable struggle for cognitive unity.

The ongoing refinement in the division of cognitive labour that an information explosion necessitates issues in a literal disintegration of knowledge. The progress of knowledge is marked by an ever-continuing proliferation of ever more restructured specialities marked by the unavoidable circumstance that any given speciality cell cannot know exactly what is going on even next door—let alone at a significant remove. Understanding of matters outside one's

---

[20] On this process see sects. 3.2 and 3.3.

immediate bailiwick is bound to become superficial. At home base one knows the details, nearby one has an understanding of generalities, but at a greater remove one can be no more than an informed amateur.

This disintegration of knowledge is also manifested vividly in the fact that our cognitive taxonomies are bursting at the seams. Consider the example of taxonomic structure of physics. In the 11th (1911) edition of the *Encyclopaedia Britannica*, physics is described as a discipline composed of nine constituent branches (e.g. 'Acoustics' or 'Electricity and Magnetism') which were themselves partitioned into twenty further specialities (e.g. 'Thermo-electricity' or 'Celestial Mechanics'). The 15th (1974) version of the *Britannica* divides physics into twelve branches whose subfields are—seemingly—too numerous for listing. (However the 14th (1960s) edition carried a special article entitled 'Physics, Articles on', which surveyed more than 130 special topics in the field.) When the National Science Foundation launched its inventory of physical specialties with the National Register of Scientific and Technical Personnel in 1954, it divided physics into twelve areas with ninety specialities. By 1970 these figures had increased to sixteen and 210, respectively.[21] And the process continues unabated to the point where people are increasingly reluctant to embark on this classifying project at all.

Substantially the same story can be told for every field of science. The emergence of new disciplines, branches, and specialties is manifest everywhere. And as though to negate this tendency and maintain unity, one finds an ongoing evolution of interdisciplinary syntheses— physical chemistry, astrophysics, biochemistry, etc. The very attempt to counteract fragmentation produces new fragments. Indeed, the phenomenology of this domain is nowadays so complex that some writers urge that the idea of a 'natural taxonomy of science' must be abandoned altogether.[22] The expansion of the scientific literature is in fact such that natural science has in recent years been disintegrating before our very eyes. An ever larger number of ever more refined specialities has made it more and more difficult for experts in a given

---

[21] *American Science Manpower: 1954–1956* (Washington: National Science Foundation Publications, 1961) and 'Specialties List for Use with 1970 National Register of Scientific and Technical Personnel' (Washington: National Science Foundation Publication, 1970).

[22] See Dupré, *The Disorder of Things*.

branch of science to achieve a thorough understanding about what is going on even in the speciality next door.

It is, of course, possible that the development of physics may eventually carry us to theoretical unification where everything that we class among the laws of nature belongs to one grand unified theory—one all-encompassing deductive systematization integrated even more tightly than that of Newton's *Principia Mathematica*.[23] But the covers of this elegantly contrived 'book of nature' will have to encompass a mass of increasingly elaborate diversity and variety. Like a tricky mathematical series, it will have to generate ever more dissimilar constituents which, despite their abstract linkage, are concretely as different as can be. And whatever convergent unification there may abstractly be at the pinnacle of a pyramid of explanatory principle, further down there will be an endlessly expansive range encompassing the most variegated components. The unity of science to which many theorists aspire may indeed come to be realized at the level of concepts and theories shared between different sciences—that is, at the level of ideational overlaps. But this is always a highly abstract unity combining a concrete mishmash of incredible variety and diversity since for every conceptual commonality and shared element there will emerge a dozen differentiations. The increasing complexity of our world-picture is a striking phenomenon throughout the development of modern science, which means that this will be an aspiration rather than an accomplished fact. It represents a goal towards which we may be able to make progress but which we will never be able to attain.[24]

Yet complexity is not an unqualified negative. It is an unavoidable concomitant of progress. We could not extend our cognitive or our practical grasp of the world without coming to terms with its complexification. Throughout the realm of human artifice—cognitive artifice included—further complexity is part and parcel of extending the frontiers of progress. The struggle with complexity that we encounter throughout our cognitive efforts is an inherent and unavoidable aspect of the human condition's progressive impetus to doing more and doing it better.

[23] See Steven Weinberg, *Dreams of a Final Theory* (New York: Pantheon, 1992). See also Edoardo Amaldi, 'The Unity of Physics', *Physics Today*, 261 (Sept. 1973), 23–9. Compare also C. F. von Weizsäcker, 'The Unity of Physics', in Ted Bastin (ed.), *Quantum Theory and Beyond* (Cambridge: Cambridge University Press, 1971).

[24] For variations on this theme see the author's *The Limits of Science* (Berkeley: University of California Press, 1984).

2.7. Nomic or Operational Complexity

The preceding discussion has focused on the world's compositional and descriptive complexity both in its synchronous and in its temporal dimensions. We shall now turn to the question of its nomic and operational complexity, shifting from issues of structure to issues of process.

In a law-hierarchy, any particular law is potentially a member of a wider family that will itself exhibit various lawful characteristics and thus be subject to synthesis under still 'higher' laws. We thus move from first-order laws governing phenomena to second-order laws governing such laws, and so on, ascending to new levels of sophistication and comparative complexity as we move along. No matter what law may be at issue, there arise new questions about it that demand an answer in emergently new lawful terms. It becomes crucial in this context that higher-level patterns are not necessarily derivable from lower-level ones. The statistical frequency with which the individual letters A and T occur in a text fails to determine the frequency with which a combination like AT occurs. (Note that the groups $ATATATAT$ and $TTTTAAAA$ both have a 50 per cent frequency of As and of Ts, yet the pair AT occurs four times in the first group but never in the second.)

On the other hand, lower-level patterns may also become lost in higher-level ones. Consider, for instance, the sequence of 0s and 1s projected according to the rule that $x_i = 1$ if a certain physical situation obtains (or is exemplified) on occasion number i, and $x_i = 0$ if not. Whenever two different features generate such sequences, say

0100110100...

1001011010...

we can introduce the corresponding *matching sequence*—namely 0010010001...—such that its i-th position is 1 if the two base sequences *agree* at their respective i-th positions, and 0 if they *disagree*. Such matching sequences will have a life of their own. And even if two base sequences are entirely random, their matching sequence need not be, for example when those random base sequences simply exchange 0s and 1s. (Even random phenomena can be related by laws of co-ordination.)

Note, moreover, that one can always regard matching sequences themselves as further base sequences, so as to yield 'second-order' phenomena, as it were. One can then proceed to examine the relationships between them—or between them and other base sequences. This process yields a potential hierarchy of 'laws of co-ordination'—at level $i + 1$ we have the laws of co-ordination between sequences at level i. Such a perspective illustrates how simple base phenomena can ramify to bring more and more grist to the mill of study and analysis. Increasingly sophisticated mechanisms of conceptual co-ordination can lead us to regard the same phenomena in the light of different complexity-levels.

These considerations indicate that quite different regularities and laws can emerge at different law-levels. Suppose, for example, a natural system to be such that for essentially technical reasons a certain parameter p cannot be evaluated by us at the precise time-point t, but only on average over an interval around t. In such a case, the system can be very simple indeed—it need contain *no* complexities apart from those at issue in the preceding assumptions—and yet the prospect of endless cognitive progress is nevertheless available. For as our capacity to make p-determinations down to smaller and smaller time-intervals increases from minutes to seconds to milliseconds to nanoseconds, and so on, we can obtain an increasingly comprehensive insight into the *modus operandi* of the system and thus obtain ever fuller information about it that could not have been predetermined on the basis of earlier knowledge. Since averages at larger levels of scale do not determine those at smaller ones, quite different modes of comportment—and thus laws—can manifest themselves with the new phenomena that arise at different levels.[25]

Or, consider a somewhat different illustration. Suppose a totally random sequence of 2s and 3s, on the order of 2 3 2 2 3 . . . And suppose further a transformation that substitutes the pair 10 for 2 and 11 for 3 so as to yield:

10 11 10 10 11 . . .

Now suppose this series to be given. We are now in a position to ascertain such 'laws' as:

[25] The variation of modes of comportment at different levels means that the descriptive taxonomies at those levels will differ also, and may well be conceptually disjoint from one another. For variations on this theme see Dupré, *The Disorder of Things*.

1. The sequence of *even-numbered* positions 01001 ... will be a random mix of 0s and 1s (which simply mirrors the initial random sequence of 2s and 3s).

2. All the *odd-numbered* positions are filled by 1s.

We confront a peculiar mixture of randomness with regularity here. But of course it is only by studying *pairs* in that given zero-one sequence that we can discern its code. Only by bringing appropriate co-ordination *concepts* to bear can we discern the laws at issue. And no matter how far we push forward along such lines into even more elaborate configurations the prospect of *further* structural laws can never be eliminated—nor downplayed by claiming that such laws are inherently less significant than the rest.

And there is no reason why this sort of nomic novelty cannot continue to recur ad infinitum. For a particular system can always exhibit new patterns of phenomenal order in its operations over time, and so there is always more to be learned about it. There is no end to the new levels of functional complexity of operation that can be investigated with such a system. Co-ordination phenomena have a life of their own. In principle, it will always be possible to discern yet further levels of lawfully structured relationship.[26] When we change the purview of our conceptual horizons, there is always in principle more to be learned—novelties of order that could not have been predicted from earlier, lower-level information. And this means, interestingly enough, that once the world is sufficiently complex in the operational mode to impose limits upon our cognitive interaction with it, then it certainly need not be infinitely complex in the compositional mode to provide for the prospect of indefinite scientific progress. God could call a halt after the seventh day and rest satisfied in the contemplation of his finished labour. Science can never afford this luxury.

2.8. The Imperfectibility of Knowledge in a Complex World

With such an unending exfoliation of law-levels, our knowledge of the world's lawful order becomes self-potentiating and new combinations can always spring up to exploit the interrelations among old

[26] On issues of complexity in science see the works of Mario Bunge, especially the *Myth of Simplicity* (Englewood Cliffs, NJ: Prentice Hall, 1963) and *Scientific Research* (2 vols.; New York: Springer, 1967).

disciplines. Given chemistry and biology we can develop biochemistry; given mathematics and astronomy, we can develop the mathematics of astronomical relationships. Wherever interfaces exist among such areas, new insights into lawful processes can be expected. And it is clear that such an endless proliferation of laws would also serve to block any prospect of completing science. There is accordingly no need to suppose that the *physical* complexity of nature need be unlimited for nature to have an unlimited cognitive depth: the ongoing *nomic* complexity of nature's laws suffices to provide for potentially endless discovery.[27]

We must thus come to terms with the fact that we cannot realistically expect that our science will ever—at *any* given stage of its actual development—be in a position to afford us more than a very partial and incomplete representation of a highly complex nature. After all, the achievement of cognitive control over nature requires not only intellectual instrumentalities (concepts, ideas, theories, knowledge) but also, and no less importantly, the deployment of physical resources (technology and 'power'), since our knowledge of nature's processes unavoidably calls for interacting with her. And the physical resources at our disposal are restricted and finite. It follows that our capacity to effect control is bound to remain imperfect and incomplete, with much in the realm of the doable always remaining undone. We shall never be able to travel down this route as we might like to go.

The Danish historian of science A. G. Drachmann closed his fine book *The Mechanical Technology of Greek and Roman Antiquity*[28] with the following observation: 'I should prefer not to seek the cause of the failure to make an invention in the social conditions till I was quite sure that it was not to be found in the technical possibilities of the time'. The history of science, as well as that of technology, is crucially conditioned by the limited nature of 'the technical possibilities of the time'. And this is as true for us as it was of the ancients.

In scientific inquiry into nature, *technological dependency sets technological limits*, first to data acquisition and then to theory projection. Every successive level of technical capability in point of observation and experimentation has its limitation through limits

[27] For an interesting and suggestive analysis of 'the architecture of complexity,' see Herbert A. Simon, *The Sciences of the Artificial* (Cambridge, Mass.: MIT Press, 1969).

[28] Madison: University of Wisconsin Press, 1963.

whose overcoming opens up yet another more sophisticated operational level of the technological state of the art. There will always be
more to be done. The accessible pressures and temperatures can
in theory always be increased, the low-temperature experiments
brought closer to absolute zero, the particles accelerated closer to
the speed of light, and so on. But when we move halfway towards that
goal the next halfway step becomes vastly more difficult. Progress is
always possible but is increasingly demanding. And experience
teaches that any such enhancement of practical mastery brings new
phenomena to view—and thereby provides an enhanced capability to
test yet further hypotheses and discriminate between alternative
theories conducive to deepening our knowledge of nature.[29]

Limitations of *physical* capacity and capability also spell *cognitive*
limitations for empirical science. Where there are inaccessible phenomena, there must be cognitive inadequacy as well. To this extent, at
any rate, the empiricists were surely right. Only the most fanatical
rationalist could uphold the capacity of sheer intellect to compensate
for the lack of data. The existence of unobserved phenomena means
that our theoretical systematizations may well be (and presumably
are) incomplete. In so far as certain phenomena are not just unde-
tected but by their very nature inaccessible (even if only for the
merely economic reasons suggested above), our theoretical knowledge of nature must be presumed imperfect. Fundamental features
inherent in the structure of man's interactive inquiry into the ways of
the world thus conspire to ensure the incompleteness of our knowledge—and moreover, will do so at any particular stage of the tech-
nological/cognitive game.

Here technological limitations carry cognitive limits in their wake.
There will always be yet unrealized interactions with nature of so
great a scale (as measured in energy, pressure, temperature, particle-
velocities, etc.) that their realization would require greater resources
than we can commit. And where there are interactions to which we
have no access, there are (presumably) phenomena that we cannot
discern. It would be very unreasonable to expect nature to confine the
distribution of cognitively significant phenomena to those ranges
that lie conveniently within our reach. But while there is always
more to be discovered, the doing of it becomes increasingly difficult
as we move into the increasingly remote regions of parametric space.

---

[29] On the implausibility of seeing physics as a unified and closed mathematical system
see Edoardo Amaldi, 'The Unity of Physics', 23–9.

And since our material resources are limited, these limits inexorably circumscribe our cognitive access to the real world.

We can plausibly estimate the amount of gold or oil yet to be discovered, because we know the earth's extent and can thus establish a proportion between what we have explored and what we have not. But we cannot comparably estimate the amount of knowledge yet to be discovered, because we have and can have no way of relating what we know to what we do not. At best, we can consider the proportion of currently envisioned questions we can in fact resolve; and this is an unsatisfactory procedure. For the very idea of cognitive limits has a paradoxical air. It suggests that we claim knowledge about something outside knowledge. But (to hark back to Hegel), with respect to the realm of knowledge, we are not in a position to draw a line between what lies inside and what lies outside—seeing that, *ex hypothesi*, we have no cognitive access to that latter. One cannot make a survey of the relative extent of our knowledge or ignorance about nature except by basing it on some overall picture or model of nature that is already in hand via prevailing science. But this is clearly an inadequate procedure. This process of judging the adequacy of our science on its own telling may be the best we can do, but it remains an essentially circular and thereby unavoidably inconclusive way of proceeding. The long and short of it is that there is no cognitively satisfactory basis for maintaining the completeness of science in a rationally cogent way. For while we can confidently anticipate that our scientific technology will see ongoing improvement in response to continued expenditure of effort, we cannot expect it ever to attain perfection. There is no reason to think that we ever will, or indeed can, reach the end of the line.

We live in a world without categorical guarantees. In various fundamental respects, our world may prove to be random and disorderly. But from a cognitive point of view this is not the worst prospect. For a random order is still an order of sorts. But anarchy— the total absence of laws—is something very different. Thus consider a series like

12112ABCBDFKxyxzzxx . . .

that consists of random-length groups of arbitrarily differentiated symbols. Here we cannot even specify the kind of thing that will be at issue. Not only is there no specifiable pattern to the specific items but there is no phenomenological order whatsoever. It is this sort of thing that is at issue with anarchy: not only cannot we predict which item will come next but we cannot even predict what *sort* of item will come next.

As best we can tell, the further we move from fundamentals to deal with additional complications with the phenomena at issue in the evolutionary series of the sciences:

physics, chemistry, biology, anthropology, psychology, economics, politics

the further we move in the direction of anarchy. And the fundamental law of nature to the effect that complexity makes for instability means that this carries us ever further to an anarchic condition of things. And anarchy is by nature a decisive impediment to the development of scientific understanding.

As far as we can ever tell there is no limit of theoretical principle—let alone of cognitive practice—to the cognitive complexity of the real. The things that populate the real world are always—both individually and in the aggregate—of an inner complexity so deep that inquiry and cognition cannot get to the bottom of it. There is always more to be done—and to be said about it. Complexity is a definitive and unavoidable feature of the real and as such has far-reaching—and profoundly humbling—implications for the nature of our knowledge.

The description and explanation of the real as best we are able to achieve it can never actually exhaust reality: adequately describing or explaining the world is a matter of aspiration and never of achievable accomplishment. And the finitude of actual knowledge in the face of the unlimited cognitive depth imposed by nature's complexity means not only that our science is always incomplete but also that it is always of questionable correctness. For new phenomena almost invariably destabilize old and constrain a readjustment in our preexisting theories. It is somewhere between unrealistic and foolish to think that we can manage to arrive at a completely definitive account of the law structure of the world.

The cognitive project like the moral project is a matter of doing the best we can in the face of a sobering realization of ultimate inadequacy. And in science as in the moral life, we can function perfectly well in the realization that perfection is unattainable. No doubt here and there a scientist may nurse the secret hope of attaining some fixed and final definitive result that will stand, untouchable and changeless, through all subsequent ages; but such unrealistic aspirations are by no means essential to the scientific enterprise as such. Here, as elsewhere, in the realm of human endeavour it is a matter of making the best possible use of the tools that lie at hand.

To be sure, the circumstance that perfection is unattainable does nothing to countervail against the no less real fact that improvement is realizable, that progress is possible. The undeniable prospect of realizable progress—of overcoming genuine defects and deficiencies that we find in the work of our predecessors—affords ample impetus to scientific innovation. Scientific progress is not only motivated *a fronte* by the pull of an unattainable ideal; it is also stimulated *a tergo* by the push of dissatisfaction with the deficiencies of achieved positions. The labours of science are doubtless sometimes pulled forward by the mirage of (unattainable) perfection. But they are less vigorously pushed onward by the (perfectly realizable) wish to do better than our predecessors in the enterprise.

There are two ways of looking at progress: as a movement away from the start, or as a movement towards the goal. On the one hand, there is advancement-progress, defined in terms of increasing distance from the starting-point. On the other hand, there is destination-progress, defined in terms of decreasing distance from the goal (the destination). With any finitely distant goal these two are equivalent—as with a foot-race, for example. But when the goal is infinitely removed, they are very different. Consider Fig. 2.1.

Here we obviously increase the distance travelled from S in exactly the same amount as we decrease the distance remaining to a definite destination D: each step further from S is a step just exactly that much closer to D. But if there is no attainable destination—if we are engaged on a journey that is, for all we know, literally endless and has no determinable destination, or only one that is infinitely distant— then we just cannot manage to decrease our distance from it. We can

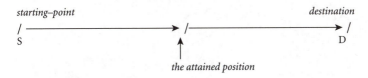

starting–point   destination

/ ——————————————————→ / ——————————————————→ /
S   D

↑
the attained position

Fig. 2.1 Structure of a journey

move further from *S* but this takes us no nearer to that now un-attainable destination. Where arrival at a definite destination is im-possible, all we can then ever do is to make advancement-progress—to make still further improvements on the already attained position. The idea of approaching an ultimate goal becomes impossible here.[30] The upshot of such deliberations is straightforward. The idea of progressively *improving* our science can be implemented without difficulty, since we can clearly improve our performance as regards its goals of prediction, control, and explanatory comprehensiveness. But the idea of *perfecting* our science cannot be implemented in an unfathomably complex world. We cannot and never will warrantedly be able to regard the attained position of science (as it exists here and now) as something finished and complete.[31]

---

[30] This consideration allays Kuhn's worries about science pursuing truth. For progress with respect to truth is something quite different from progress towards *the truth*. (See Thomas Kuhn, *The Structure of Scientific Revolutions* (Chicago: University of Chicago Press, 1962.)

[31] For other aspects of this chapter's deliberations see the author's *Scientific Progress* (Oxford: Blackwell, 1976) and *Limits of Science* (Berkeley: University of California Press, 1985).

3

Order in Nature, Multifaceted Reality, and Contextualistic Realism

SYNOPSIS

(1) We can learn about nature only by interactively pushing up against it, and what it is that it yields to us will depend on how hard we push. (2) Our view of the world accordingly changes in the course of techno-logy-induced scientific progress. (3) The picture of nature we obtain at one level of observational and experimental sophistication becomes destabilized at the next level. (4) With scientific progress we constantly have to reconstruct the concept mechanisms we use in science. (5) Order can emerge from blurring, and added detail can readily destroy an earlier order. (6) In theory there is the prospect that all the laws of physics as presently conceived are the product of a blurring that dissolves into disorder at a level of sufficiently fine-grained detail. (7) The question of what physical nature is really like thus may well not admit of a uniform reply but require the contextual response, 'Nature is thus-and-so at a particular—and potentially ever-changing—level of invest-igative sophistication.' And this perspective throws a dark shadow across the prospects of a scientific realism that holds that nature actually is as current or even future science claims it to be.

3.1. Newton's Third Law as an Epistemological Principle in Physical Inquiry

There is good reason to think that the way in which research in physics proceeds itself canalizes and limits the interpretation that can reasonably be placed upon its findings regarding the nature of the physical world. In particular, it will be argued here that there are

The material of this chapter formed the core of the first Christian Wolff Lecture that I delivered at the University of Marburg in July 1999.

marked limits to scientific realism if this doctrine is construed as maintaining that the natural world actually is as natural science depicts it as being. For if we are going to be realistic about it (in the *other* sense of the term) then we must acknowledge that the very nature of physical inquiry as we actually pursue it as a human practice is such as to render this thesis very questionable.

First a methodological preliminary. It was Hegel's great merit to have brought the factor of history into the forefront of philosophy, constraining philosophers to recognize that human knowledge in general—and our knowledge about the natural world in particular—has to be viewed as a dynamical system that is changing and developing over time through the efforts of historical individuals. Contemporary epistemologists have accordingly been much exercised with the question of what this fact of the historicity of knowledge as an ever-changing artefact teaches us about the nature of knowledge. The present discussion will take a cognate but somewhat different line, however. Its procedure is to give the issue a peculiarly philosophy-of-science twist by asking: 'What does the very fact that human knowledge of nature has developed as it has teach us about the nature of physical reality?'

Natural science is not a fixed object, a finished product of inquiries, but an ongoing process. In developing natural science, we humans began by exploring the world in our own locality, and not just our *spatial* neighbourhood but—more far-reachingly—our *parametric* neighbourhood in the 'space' of physical variables defined by such variables as temperature, pressure, and electric charge. Near the home-base of the state of things in our accustomed natural environment, we can operate with relative ease and freedom—thanks to the evolutionary attunement of our sensory and cognitive apparatus—in scanning nature with the unassisted senses for data regarding its modes of operation. But in due course we accomplish everything that can be managed by these straightforward means. To do more, we have to explore further—to extend our probes into nature more deeply, deploying increasing technical sophistication to achieve more and more demanding levels of interactive capability, moving ever further away from our evolutionary home-base in nature toward increasingly remote observational frontiers. From the egocentric starting-point of our local region of parameter space, we journey ever more distantly outwards to explore nature's various parametric dimensions.

Newton's third law also operates as an epistemological principle, and here too action equals reaction (*actio = reactio*). Pushing nature with increasingly powerful observational and experimental technology forces her to yield up new phenomena to our inspection. Everything depends on just how *and how hard* we can push against nature in situations of observational and detectional interaction. And we cannot achieve the ultimacy of definite laws where nature is concerned, seeing that nature always has hidden reserves of power that hold surprises in store for us.

Science, the cognitive exploration of the ways of the world, is a matter of the interaction of the human mind with nature—of the mind's cognitive exploitation of the data to which it gains access in order to penetrate the secrets of nature. The crucial fact is that scientific progress hinges not just on the structure of nature itself but also on the character of the information-acquiring processes by which we investigate it.

In cultivating scientific inquiry, we scan nature for interesting phenomena and then elaborate whatever useful regularities they may suggest. As a fundamentally inductive process, scientific theorizing calls for devising the least complex theory structure capable of accommodating the available data. At each stage we try to embed the phenomena and their regularities within the simplest (cognitively most efficient) explanatory structure able to answer our questions about the world and to guide our interactions in it. But the natural dialectic of the process puts ever greater demands upon us, as regards both the scope of our data and the sophistication of our theories.

To extend our search for cognitively significant phenomena we have to increase the available magnification (very generally understood) that is made available by our observational and experimental technology to examine nature in fuller detail, as it were. But step by step as the process advances we are driven to meeting further, ever greater demands which can be met only with a yet more powerful technology of data exploration and management. And as the range of telescopes, the energy of particle accelerators, the effectiveness of low-temperature apparatus, the potency of pressurization equipment, the power of vacuum-creating contrivances, and the accuracy of measurement apparatus increases, our capacity to probe more deeply into the parametric space of the physical world is enhanced. And progressively greater power, greater capacity in these regards means that we can look ever more deeply into nature's *modus operandi*. Such enlarged access brings new phenomena to light, and the examination and theoretical accommodation of these phenomena is the basis for growth in our scientific understanding of nature.

The key to the great progress of contemporary physics accordingly lies in the enormous strides which an ever more sophisticated scientific technology has made possible through enlarging the observational and experimental basis of our theoretical knowledge of natural processes. Francis Bacon's classic precept obtains: 'Human knowledge and power are coextensive' (*Scientia et potentia humana in idem coincidunt*).[1] The idea is that enhancing the sophistication of man–nature interaction enables us to increase our cognitive magnification—to see nature, as it were, at increasing levels of detail. And phenomenological novelty is seemingly inexhaustible: we can never feel confident that we have got to the bottom of it: given our limited capacities we can never get to the bottom of it. Nature always has fresh reserves of phenomena at her disposal. But scientific innovation becomes more and more difficult—and expensive—as we push our explorations even further away from our evolutionary home-base toward increasingly remote frontiers of parametric space.

Without an ever-developing technology, scientific progress would soon grind to a halt. The discoveries of today cannot be made with yesterday's equipment and techniques. To conduct new experiments, to secure new observations, and to detect new phenomena, an ever more powerful investigative technology is needed. Scientific progress depends crucially and unavoidably on our technical capability to penetrate into the increasingly deeper—and increasingly difficult—reaches of physical detail.

This picture is not, of course, one of *geographical* exploration but rather of the physical exploration—and subsequent theoretical systematization—of phenomena distributed over the parametric space of the physical quantities spreading out all about us in nature. This approach in terms of exploration provides a conception of scientific research as a prospecting search for the new phenomena demanded by significant new scientific findings. The key to the great progress of contemporary physics lies in the enormous strides in technological capability.[2] It is of the very essence of the enterprise that progress in

---

[1] Francis Bacon, *Novum organum*, bk. I, sect. iii.

[2] A homely fishing analogy of Sir Arthur Eddington's is useful here. He saw the experimentalists as akin to a fisherman who trawls nature with the net of his equipment for detection and observation. Now suppose (says Eddington) that a fisherman trawls the

natural science requires entry into ever more remote reaches of parametric space.

The progress of natural science as we know it thus embarks us on a literally endless endeavour to improve the range of effective experimental intervention, because only by operating under new and heretofore inaccessible conditions of observational or experimental systemization—attaining extreme temperature, pressure, particle velocity, field strength, and so on—can we realize situations that enable us to put knowledge-expanding hypotheses and theories to the test. The enormous power, sensitivity, and complexity deployed in present-day experimental science have not been sought for their own sake but rather because the research frontier has moved on into an area where this sophistication is the indispensable requisite of further progress. In science, as in war, the battles of the present cannot be fought effectively with the armament of the past.

3.2. A Changing Landscape: Things Look Different at Different Levels of Detail

Successive stages in enhancing the power and sophistication of the technological state of the art of scientific inquiry lead us to ever-different views about the make-up of physical reality and its laws.

As Bacon saw, nature will never tell us more than we can forcibly extract from her. And at the successive levels of interaction—of technical sophistication, as it were—we can subject nature to successively deeper probes. And all historical experience at our disposal indicates that as this process unfolds nature will wear a steadily changing aspect. At every state-of-the-art stage of technological capability we encounter a different order or aspect of things. And the reason why nature exhibits different aspects at different levels is not that nature herself is somehow stratified and has different levels of being or of operation but rather that what we find is bound to reflect the apposite technology of observation; it is always something that depends on the mechanisms by which we search. For the phenomena

seas using a fishnet of 2-inch mesh. Then fish of a smaller size will simply go uncaught, and those who analyse the catch will accordingly have an incomplete and distorted view of aquatic life. The situation in science is the same. Only by improving our observational means of trawling nature can such imperfections be mitigated. (See A. S. Eddington, *The Nature of the Physical World* (Cambridge: Cambridge University Press, 1928).)

we are able to detect will depend not merely on nature's doings alone, but on the power of the physical and conceptual instruments that we ourselves use in probing nature.

On a map of the USA, Chicago is but a dot. But when we go to a map of Illinois it begins to take on some substance, and on a map of Cook County it presents a substantial and characteristic shape. But this is not the end of the story. We could, in theory, go on to map it block by block, house by house, room by room, dish by pitcher. And with increasing detail new and different features constantly emerge. Science is like that. Where does the process stop? Not with atoms, certainly—for the impenetrable and unchanging atoms of the ancient Greeks have become increasingly dematerialized and ethereal. As we increase the power of our particle accelerators, our view of the make-up of the subatomic realm becomes not only ever different but also ever stranger. And the possibility of change is to all practical intents and purposes unending.[3]

As we proceed along this route of an increasingly sophisticated and extensive examination of the observationally accessible phenomena, journeying more extensively through nature's parameter space with increasing technical sophistication, the scene that confronts us is ever changing. It is by no means the case that we see the same sorts of things—nor that we continue seeing the old things in the same sort of way. Quite different regularities and laws can emerge at different levels of sophistication in the handling of details. And in principle, there is an ever-present prospect of discerning yet further levels of lawfully structured relationship.[4]

We thus arrive at:

THESIS 1: Nature is able to exhibit a different face—display different laws, categories, modes of order—when considered at different levels of detail.

In elucidating this thesis, it will prove helpful to consider an analogy. Let us suppose that we investigate some domain of phenomena along

[3] On the issues of this section see the author's *Scientific Progress* (Oxford: Blackwell, 1978) and *Scientific Realism* (Dordrecht: D. Reidel, 1987). A fascinating treatment of relevant issues is offered in Michael Redhead, *From Physics to Metaphysics* (Cambridge: Cambridge University Press, 1995), especially the final chapter.

[4] On issues of complexity in science see Mario Bunge, *Myth of Simplicity* (Englewood Cliffs, NJ: Prentice Hall, 1963) and *Scientific Research* (2 vols.; New York: Springer, 1967); Klaus Mainzer, *Thinking in Complexity* (Berlin: Springer, 1997); as well as the author's *Complexity* (New Brunswick, NJ: Transaction Publishers, 1998).

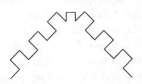

FIG. **3.1** A first-level regularity

FIG. **3.2** A second-level regularity

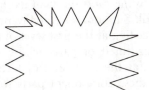

FIG. **3.3** A third-level regularity

these lines and that in the first instance the picture we arrive at presents a certain sort of regularity (Fig. 3.1).

We say: 'Aha, this sector of the world's processes proceeds in the manner of a mountain range.' But at the next level we investigate those zigzags more closely. We note now that they have the distinctly more complex form shown at Fig. 3.2.

We say: 'So—we did not quite have it right to begin with. This sector of the world's processes actually has the character of fluctuating castellations.' And so, at the next level we investigate those castellations more closely. We now note that they in turn have changed form (Fig. 3.3).

We now say: 'Aha, this sector of the world is made up of regularly configured zig-zags.' And so this sort of observation-driven revisionism continues at every successive stage of further technological sophistication in our experimental and observational interactions with physical nature. At every level of detail nature's apparent *modus operandi* looks very different and its governing regularities take on an aspect markedly different from what went before and crucially disparate from it.

Presumably at each stage we can readily comprehend and explain the situation obtaining at the earlier stages. We can always say, 'Yes, of course, given that that is how things stand, it is quite understandable that earlier on, when we proceeded in such-and-such a cruder way, we arrived at the sort of findings we did—inadequate and inaccurate though they are.' But this wisdom is clearly one of hindsight only. At no stage do we have the prospect of using *foresight* to predict what lies ahead. The impossibility of foreseeing the new phenomena that await us means that at no point can we prejudge what lies further down the explanatory road. We have no prospect of being able to discern the future's view of nature's laws.

Let us now turn from a concern with the *lawful comportment* of the world's phenomena to the *constitution* of its things. An analogy will once again be helpful. Suppose we initially investigate objects of a certain type *X*. Proceeding at the first level of sophistication we see these objects as constituted of parts whose structure is dot-like. Closer investigation (at the next level of technical sophistication) leads us to see that these component parts were not actually solid dot-like units at all, but clusters of small specks. And when we investigate further it emerges that the component specks that constitute these clusters are themselves in fact clouds of smaller units that have a rectangular form. And so on. As this analogy indicates, physical nature can—as the history of science in fact indicates that it does—have very different aspects when viewed from the vantage points of different levels of sophistication in the technology of nature–investigator interactions. The fact is that as regards both the observable *regularities* of nature and the discernible *constituents* of nature, very different results emerge at the various levels of the observational state of the art. As we study it at different levels of detail by increasing our investigative magnification, nature presents us with an ever-changing panorama of phenomena and of laws—much in the manner of the previous analogies. And there is, as best we can tell, no limit to the world's ever-increasing complexity that comes with our ever-increasing grasp of its detail.[5]

---

[5] To be sure, some recent thinking in quantum theory inclines to holding that physical structure does not continue downwards infinitely in its intricacy with all structure eventually blurring out (at the Planck length of 10 exp − 33 cm. if not before). (See V. L. Ginzberg, *Key Problems of Physics and Astrophysics*, tr. O Glevov (Moscow: MIR Publishing House, 1978), 66–9. However, the structure at issue here is a *spatial* structure. The finitude of the nomic structure of matter's lawful comportment does not follow.

The history of physics affords a sequence of episodes of leaping to the wrong conclusions because new observational findings progressively indicate that matters are not quite so simple as heretofore thought. As ample experience indicates, our ideas about nature are subject to contrived changes of mind with respect to the *modus operandi* of things as we explore parametric space more extensively. The technologically mediated entry into new regions of parameter space constantly destabilizes the previously attained equilibrium between data and theory by bringing new phenomena to view. In the course of its technical progress, science presents us with a picture of nature that is ever-changing in its details.

3.3. Destabilization

As the line of thought we have been following indicates, technological progress constantly enlarges the window through which we look out upon nature's parametric space. In developing natural science we continually enlarge our view of this space and then generalize upon what we see. But the technologically mediated entry into new regions of parameter space constantly brings new phenomena to view in a way that destabilizes the attained equilibrium between data and theory. Historical experience shows that there is every reason to expect that our ideas about nature are subject to constant radical changes as we explore its deeper structure in greater detail. And it does not require a sophisticated knowledge of history of science to realize that our worst fears are usually realized—that our theories seldom if ever survive intact in the wake of substantial extensions in our cognitive access to the new phenomena of the previously inaccessible sectors of nature's parametric space.

In proceeding through such an unending exfoliation of levels of magnification, our knowledge of the world's lawful order is never secure. In particular, we have the following:

THESIS 2: The natural laws that we find to obtain in considering nature at one level of detail may—and generally do—become unravelled (abolished, deconstructed) at a greater level of detail.

As our technology-mediated explanation of nature's parameter space improves, things no longer continue to look the same. What we have here is not a homogeneous lunar landscape, where once we have seen one sector we have seen it all, and where theory projections from lesser data generally remain in place when further data comes our way. To be sure, it could, in theory, possibly occur that just exactly the same relationship-patterns simply recur from level to level—that the patterns of phenomena that we encounter at level $i + 1$ simply reduplicate those already met with at level i. (This is the functional equivalent at the nomic level of the recurrence of physical patterns at different levels of scale characterizing the 'fractal' structures made prominent by E. Mandelbrot.) However, this is a very special case that need not and will not obtain across the board. Science as we have it in all its branches indicates there is no good reason to think that our world is fractal in the structure of its natural processes—that nothing new ever arises as we move on to consider things in greater detail. There is no warrant for assuming an end to such a sequence of levels of integrative complexity of phenomenal order. Each successive level of operational or functional complexity can in principle exhibit a characteristic order of its own. The phenomena we attain at the nth level here can have features whose investigation takes us to the $(n + 1)$th. New phenomena and new laws can in theory arise at every level of integrative order. The different facets of nature can generate conceptually new strata of productive operation to yield a potentially unending sequence of levels, each giving rise to its own characteristic principles of organization, themselves quite unpredictable from the standpoint of the other levels.

What is being envisioned here is a technology-driven view of physical science subject to the idea that major advances in the observational and experimental technology in any given area of physical science invariably leads—somewhere along the line—to the detection of phenomena that constrain substantial revisions on the side of theory. The crux is that the theory/data equilibrium that we achieve at any given state-of-the-art stage of scientific technology is always unstable and becomes disestablished as the power and capacity of the relevant technology increase.

3.4. Deconstruction and Reconstruction

The data-base improvements that come in the wake of more powerful equipment instrumentation generally constrain concept changes that ramify into the realm of theory as well.

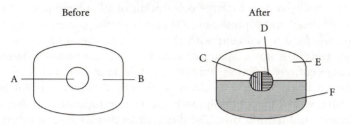

Fig. 3.4 An illustration of concept sophistication

Examine the relationships depicted in Fig. 3.4. The initial situation is given at the left and conveys a neat bit of general information: All As are Bs. (The letters indicate the thing-types or categories that are in play.) But now suppose that we were more sophisticated and confronted the later situation at the right of the figure. Here we abandon those crude As and Bs altogether like 'the cause of headaches'—they become dissolved into a plurality and no longer exist as such. Instead we now have to deal with the more sophisticated fourfold concept-manifold C, D, E, F. At this point no category-connective lawful generalization whatever will obtain. Irrespective of how we try to fit these four categories into the schema 'All Xs are Ys', no acceptable positive thesis will result. (We might indeed have it that 'All C + D are E + F, but now neither C + D nor E + F will/may any longer be a *natural kind*, since both may involve mixing apples and oranges. This sort of thing is just not an appropriate way of talking. And so at the level of the more sophisticated division no positive lawful relationship will obtain. (Only negative relationships such as 'No C is D' will hold.) The limits and laws involved are incommunicable. The situation is such that only by being crude about it and ignoring the (conceivably quite important) differences between C-D and E-F respectively, will we be able to utter a tenable affirmative generalization about these groups. Seen from the later perspective of greater sophistication we are able to see that the earlier law, 'All As are Bs'—albeit adequate enough in it own way—could only prevail by conflating (infusing, running together) the Cs and the Ds on the one hand and the Es and the Fs on the other. There can be facts that come into being only with a neglect of different facts whose very existence as such hinges on being indifferent to or oblivious of certain other more detailed and sophisticated facts. And when this neglect is overcome through further information, the facts in question become unravelled.

The reality of it is that the description of the phenomena at one level of detail and sophistication is often—perhaps even generally—*conceptually discontinuous* with that which is operative at another level. Here it is not a matter of viewing the same things differently because entirely different 'things' are at issue at different levels. At different levels we have to do with entirely different concept perspective: with different thing-kinds and taxonomies and also terms of reference and natural laws. The different levels may be connected by way of causal explanation (there may be causal correlations) but not by way of hermetical explanations (there are no conceptual connections). To re-emphasize: different levels of understanding can prove to be conceptually disjoint or discontinuous—the phenomena at issue in the one cannot in general be descriptively characterized by means (or terms) of the vocabulary appropriate to the other, with the result that at the greater level of sophistication we have to abandon any serious commitment to the concepts and the laws operative at the lesser. Like 'sunrises' and 'choleric temperaments' they become mere figures of speech.

The descriptive phenomenology of these different levels may be connected in the language of causality (there may be causal correlations) but not by way of hermeneutical explanations—there are no *conceptual* connections that enable discourse at one level to be effectively translated into the other. Different levels of understanding are conceptually incommensurable—the phenomena at issue in the one cannot be descriptively characterized by means (or in terms) of the vocabulary appropriate to the other. At the cutting-edge frontier of science things constantly take on a significantly different appearance.

This state of things has interesting implications.

3.5. Order from Blurring—from Obliviousness of Detail

The other side of the coin of the preceding deliberations is that even as the introduction of greater detail can dissolve order so the neglect of detail can generate it. We thus have to come to terms with the following idea:

THESIS 3: Order can emerge from disorder by 'blurring'—that is, by ignoring detail.

Added sensitivity and sophistication of distinctions can readily unravel significantly informative relationships. Added precision need not produce a gain in knowledge but on the contrary can issue in a cognitive loss by deconstructing descriptive categorizations and undoing lawful regularities. Cognizance of detail can tie our tongues. Only by ignoring some potentially large differences in accent and mode of speech can we say that the different speakers have spoken the same sentence. Only by resolutely ignoring a vast manifold of differences can one speak generally of hardware, or of trees, or of elements.

Consider the eminently lawful series:

PQPQPQPQ...

This series is very simply described as a succession of PQs. But now suppose the Ps to be 'sophisticated' into the LMs and the MOs, and the Qs to be comparably divided into MLs and LOs. And suppose further that the divisions at issue occur more or less randomly. Then the actual situation may then turn out to be something like

MOMLLMLOLMML...

which may turn out to be a close-to-random series of L-M-Os. The elegantly lawful order of the initial series has been unravelled by the newly introduced conceptual sophistication that has been brought upon the scene. Only through a neglect of the potentially significant difference between LM and MO on the one hand and ML and LO on the other was that initial order realized.

The lesson is clear. Obliviousness to distinctions can readily result in sorts of lawful regularity that become unavailable in the complexity created by greater sophistication. The fact is that in various sorts of cases lawful order can be a product of blurring and neglecting detail. Those laws may emerge only at certain levels of aggregation on the basis of an obliviousness of difference. The optician's chart may be a random succession of letters, but if your vision is blurred and they all look like Z to you a beautiful regularity will result. In the eyes of the beholder patterns of order can emerge from disorder as clouds that look like a flock of fluffy sheep emerge from a chaotic conflux of minute water particles.

We thus face the significant prospect that even when there is disorder (or even lawless anarchy) at the level of microlevel detail, lawfulness can nevertheless emerge as a phenomenon of conflation and detail-abstractive myopia. Empirically discoverable order may well prove to be a matter of incapacity in responding to details—a mere artefact of indifference or ignorance. And while such blurring can of course be in the eye of the beholder, it need not be so. That is, it need not necessarily be a *mind* that fails to respond differently to two different sets of things, virtually any sort of responsive mechanism may fail to do that. Thus when a coin machine fails to differentiate between old-style American and Canadian currency a vast manifold of economic and legal distinctions is effectively set at naught. Respondents that are indifferent to differences—that simply ignore them—may find themselves transforming a disorderly environment into a harmonious realm of manageable order.

As this example suggests, the order produced by an information-processing resource may well lie in its own *modus operandi* rather than in the nature of the materials with which it works. Suppose, for example, that we have a scanner reading a random series of 0s and 1s. But it is rather sluggish and sleepy, as it were, and only becomes alert when there are changes, thus only taking note of numbers that are new and different in relation to what has gone before. It will then transform the random series

    0010110011101001...

into

    0101010101...

That initial random series has now transmuted into an orderly series of alternating 0s and 1s. There is now elegant order, but it is only an artefact of inattention.

There are two well-known ways in which a macro-order can arise from a microlevel from which order is absent. One is by statistical aggregation of chance microlevel fluctuations (as randomly moving particles can give rise to an aggregate order subject to the gas laws). And a second is through the macro-evolution of a micro-chaos that produces orderly behaviour at a larger level, like the eddies of cigarette smoke. But we now see that there is also a third way of extracting order from disorder—namely the route of incapacity or indifference. Order is now not a matter of statistical aggregation but of *difference-suppressive blurring* of detail. And once we recognize that information-acquisition is as a matter of interaction between nature's processes and the technology of observation, it must be realized as entirely possible for a sufficiently myopic perceiver—one who is simply unable to see the disorderly details—to perceive a disorderly environment as vastly more orderly and lawful.

The sort of thing that is at issue here can be illustrated by a simple example. Consider newspaper pictures produced by means of the old dot-assemblage technology. But now suppose that the dots themselves were not solid blobs but only an agglomeration of still smaller dots. Of course at this second, deeper level all detail will be irrelevant (or at most only statistically relevant) for the base-level phenomena. The same picture will emerge irrespective of microlevel detail. Let 'supervenience' be understood in the usual way, so that Bs supervene upon the As in that if the As were different, the Bs would be different. Then what we have in view here is a *loose supervenience* based on a very loose coupling that has a great amount of slack. What such cases involve is not total but substantial indifference (invariance): only if the As were *vastly* different would the Bs be different. The sort of order that prevails on the more detailed level may be relevant to the order that emerges at the phenomenological level of lesser detail. It is this sort of situation that confronts us in the cases we have in view: the facts that obtain at one level of consideration are only very loosely geared to the facts that obtain when at the other more detailed (or more 'fundamental') level.

Of course what we need to do for present purposes is to shift from levels of scale to levels of consideration—to *conceptual* points of view in line with different degrees of cognitive sophistication. And we realize that in making the shift to greater detail we may well lose information that was, in its own way, adequate enough. For—as we have seen—information at the grosser (molar) level may well be lost when we shift to the more sophisticated level of greater fine-grained detail. The 'advance' achieved in the wake of 'superior' knowledge can be—and often is—purchased only at a substantial cognitive loss. If we dwell on the insight that a social group embodies no more than the individuals that constitute it and insist on attending only to what we can secure from the microeconomics of individual behaviour we lose at one blow virtually the whole of the useful lessons that macroeconomics makes available.

From the angle of information processing, the reality of it is that we have:

THESIS 4: Heed of detail generally complicates matters

What appears as a single phenomenon at one level of consideration can—and frequently does—dissolve into a variety of very different processes at a deeper (i.e. more sophisticated) level of consideration (as is the case in medicine with the headache or the common cold, or in chemistry with isotopes of the same element). Sometimes, it is true, added sophistication leads to consolidation and unification. On closer inspection, both coal and diamond turn out to be different versions of one basic material: carbon. But in reality added sophistication generally makes for added complication. Rarely does added detail serve to unify rather than differentiate. As things stand in the realm of inquiry, fuller inspection generally brings differences to light. The more closely and comprehensively we examine things the more elaborately we are drawn to distinguish between them. In innumerable instances casual inspection will overlook the differences that closer and more sophisticated examination reveals —differences so crucial that with respect to them, as with respect to the elephant of the storied sages, incomplete means incorrect.

3.6. A Daunting Prospect

It is tempting on first thought to accept the idea that we secure more—and indeed more useful and more reliable—information by examining matters in greater precision and detail. And this is often so. But the reality is that this is not necessarily the case. It is entirely possible that the sort of information we need or want is available at our 'natural' level of operation but comes to be dissolved in the wake of greater sophistication. Consider just one rather crude analogy. It is only with ignorance or indifference—only through neglecting all the endless possibilities for constructing chairs and the endless possibilities of placing oneself upon them—that one can secure items of knowledge on the order of 'chairs are seats'. This is a claim that we all understand at the level of folk communication in ordinary language about physical objects, but where it is not possible to conceive of an overall way to reintroduce this claim in the deeper language of physics. And this sort of situation can lead to the paradoxical result that knowledge—with its concern for the discernment of order— may in various circumstances be rooted in ignorance—namely a neglect of detail that gives rise to a discernible order that would not be available in its absence.

At the successive levels of magnification we perceive reality in increasingly fine detail—up to a point. For we always come up against limits and meet with minimally perceptible units of observation. But these are not necessarily natural units of physical existence as per the sequence: organ, cell, molecule, atom, subatomic particle. Indeed, they need not be units of physical reality at all. When we make our measurements in more detail, moving from mileposts to yardsticks to micrometres, we do indeed have to deal with different sorts of objects. But these need not be physical entities or natural units at all: their unity may well be simply a matter of our conceptualizing convenience. The objects we encounter and the laws that govern their comportment may in fact simply be artefacts of our own *modus operandi*—such as degrees of latitude and longitude.

In this regard we have to come to terms with the fact represented by the following:

THESIS 5: It is a perfectly possible prospect that irrespective of how lawful nature is at the level of lesser detail at which we operate here and now, those natural laws—as best we can currently determine them—*always* become unravelled as investigation proceeds to the more fine-grained situation of a further level of detail. Those laws as we have them often need to be changed—that is, replaced by something better.

Let us thus introduce, by way of a rather radical hypothesis, the idea of a *hierarchically law-unstable universe*—one that brings altogether different laws to view at different levels of investigative sophistication. Such a world is not an *anarchy* that lacks laws altogether—on the contrary, it has (if anything) too many laws, one for every level of consideration (albeit always different ones of different levels). What we have here is a world that can be viewed at different levels of detail and sophistication, but where laws that obtain at any given level of detail always and exceptionlessly become unstuck at the next level, seen as based on oversimplifications and misunderstandings. In such a world there are no stable natural kinds: any natural kind encountered at level i is no longer tenable as such at level $i + 1$. The order detectable at any level of detail becomes deconstructed at the next—replaced by something altogether different and conceptually incommensurable. Laws there still are, but laws that have to be conceptualized in an entirely different manner as level-correlative rather than a reflection of deeper-level laws.

Consider just one possible illustration of this line of thought: the behavioural psychology of individual humans. It is, so one could argue, altogether possible that the underlying processes—be they brain psychological or mind proto-psychological—are so complex and diversified that no discernible lawful regularities exist at the deepest levels. The *modus operandi* of individuals is so convoluted that no psychologically relevant microprocesses are universally shared by all individuals alike. Yet nevertheless at the cruder macro-level of molar human action and interaction—the level of folk psychology—lawful regularities may well become discernible and cognitively manageable.[6]

The position at issue here differs significantly from that maintained in Nancy Cartwright's provocative book on *How the Laws of Physics Lie*.[7] The relevant sector of Cartwright's position may be paraphrased as follows: Reality is too complex to be captured by our physical laws. These laws only constrain and canalize the observable phenomena, but do not exactly determine them (not even statistically). Our laws always oversimplify; they never yield more than approximations of reality. Nature is too messy, too complex and variegated, to be determined ('governed') by the laws that we can manage to formulate with the symbolic resources at our disposal.[8]

It would be the natural upshot of such a position that as we look more closely and fully at nature as the range of phenomenological detail at our disposal increases the more we have to readjust—to fine tune and revamp—our laws of nature to get them to fit reality (to 'save the phenomena'), or rather to fit fully and adequately to the range of phenomena at our cognitive disposal.

But this situation can also be viewed from a perspective rather different from that of Cartwright. Its lesson can be read as saying not that those laws of nature of ours lie because they are at variance to reality, but rather that they are in a way correct enough, accurate, and adequate to reality viewed at a *certain particular level of sophistication*

[6] On the claim that folk psychology becomes unravelled at the deeper level of scientific understanding at issue with a neurophysiological or a computational view of 'neural processes' see Paul Churchland's paper 'Eliminative Materialism and Propositional Attitudes', *Journal of Philosophy*, 78 (1983); Stephen Stich, *From Folk Psychology to Cognitive Science: The Case Against Belief* (Cambridge, Mass.: MIT Press, 1983); and Patricia Churchland, *Neurophilosophy: Towards a Unified Theory of the Mind-Brain* (Cambridge, Mass.: MIT Press, 1986).

[7] Oxford: Clarendon Press, 1983.

[8] Ibid. 49, 128–9, 159–60.

in observational and experimental technology and the concept-manifold associates therewith. To be sure this does not say that they are flat-out true, but only that they are indistinguishable from actual reality when this is viewed from a certain observational perspective—that they meet all the qualifying conditions we can reasonably impose for acknowledgment of truth at a certain level of technical competency. And as if such law-instability were not bad enough, the prospect of an even less benign sort of situation looms up before us.

THESIS 6: Conceivably *all* the physical world's lawfulness—at any and every given level of observational detail—is the product of blurring, with all the laws that we secure at that level eventually being unstable as we enhance our mastery of detail.

On such a view the lawfulness of nature is—shocking to say!—merely an artefact of inquiry. For it poses the daunting prospect that *every* supposedly general truth about the world—every so-called law of nature—may prove to be an artefact of the mode of consideration geared to a certain level of response—a level of detail that is correlative to a creature operating at a particular level of investigative technology with its particular observational and theoretical resources.

To be sure, an objector will ask, 'What of the enormous precision of the mathematical structure of natural law—does this not show that the order we envision must exist in nature as such?' Yes and no. It does indeed show that there must be a great deal of local order in the processing of nature-supplied materials, but it does nothing to show that the outcome is a matter of input rather than output. The sausage machine whose output is precision-shaped sausages need not operate on raw materials that are precise in their own make-up and shaping.

Not that such a cognitively law-unstable world need itself be lawlessly anarchic. The problem here is not a lack of laws, but the fact that there can be too many of them—with different and possibly discordant laws confronting us at different levels of investigative sophistication. As ample historical experience indicates, the scientific frontier presents us with an ever-changing terrain.

3.7. A Many-Levelled Reality

The multilevel view of nature being contemplated here has far-reaching implications for our knowledge of it. Whatever the determinable character of a series of phenomena that we examine may be, we can never rule out the possibility that yet further patterns of relationship exist. For there will be patterns of phenomena, and patterns of such patterns, and patterns of patterns of such patterns—and on and on. We can study letter sequences as such, or move on to the level of words, and thence to sentences, and thence to paragraphs, and so to chapters, to books, to book-categories, to book systems (as with French v. Chinese literature), etc. Every new level of consideration will afford phenomena of its own that will themselves admit of further study and analysis. With ongoing progress in the accession of information, inquiry will always in principle find new grist for its mill among the phenomena arising at higher levels of sophistication.

After all, even a system that is finitely complex *both* in its physical make-up *and* in its basic law structure might nevertheless yet be infinitely complex in its *productive operations* over time. A limited producer might well engender unlimited products. (There is effectively no end to the different games of chess that can be played with the same pieces and the same rules.) Even were the number of constituents of nature to be small, the ways in which they can be combined to yield products in space-time might yet be infinitely varied. Think here of the examples of letters: syllables: words: sentences: paragraphs: books: genres (novels, reference books, etc.): libraries: library systems. Even an otherwise finite nature can, like a typewriter with a limited keyboard, yield an endlessly varied text over time. It can produce a steady stream of new macro-phenomena—'new' not necessarily in kind but in their functional interrelationships and thereby in their implications for theory, so that our knowledge of nature's operations can continually be enhanced and deepened.[9] Even a world that is relatively simple in point of basic operations may well exhibit an effectively infinite *cognitive* depth when one proceeds to broaden one's notion of a natural phenomenon to include not just the processes themselves and the products that they produce, but also the relationships among them.

And there is no warrant for assuming an end to such a sequence of levels of integrative complexity of phenomenal order. Each successive level of operational or functional complexity can in principle exhibit a characteristic order of its own. The phenomena we attain at any

---

[9] Francis Bacon invoked an Alphabet of Nature analogy to argue that (theoretical) science might be completed in a few years. Nowadays this hardly seems convincing.

given level here can have features whose investigation takes us to the next level of sophistication. New phenomena and new laws can in theory arise at every level of integrative order. The different facets of nature can generate conceptually new strata of productive operation to yield a potentially unending sequence of levels, each giving rise to its own characteristic principles of organization, themselves quite unpredictable from the standpoint of the other levels. The question, 'What is physical nature really like?' may well not admit of a specific reply but require the nuanced response, 'Nature is thus-and-so at such-and-such a particular—and potentially improvable—level of investigative sophistication.'

Metaphysical realism maintains investigation-antecedently *that* there is a physical state of natural reality, and scientific realism maintains investigation-consequently that science shows us *what* this state is like. But what the present deliberations suggest is that thus 'what reality is like' is nothing definitive and categorical but something contextual and limited to a particular state-of-the-art level of sophistication in point of scientific technology.

However the element of variability that enters here is emphatically not something that authorizes an indifferentist relativism. In the context of a given investigative level things are just exactly and objectively as our inquiries at that level show them to be. Thinkers who wish to set limits to cognitive relativism are wont to employ the distinction between where we look and what we find when we look there. The former is indeed a more or less unfettered human choice, while the latter is something that is fixed and observer-independently determined once the former is resolved. However, another parameter also enters into the situation, no only where we look but *how* we look—i.e. the technology of observation and experimentation that we employ. This too is something over which we have control, but whose outcome, of course, is once again determined not by us but by the nature of things. We propose but reality disposes; we may determine the process but the product is then up to an us-independent manifold of physical reality. The upshot of our approach is accordingly not relativism but a contextualistic realism—a realism, that is to say, that sees 'truth about reality' as accessible in a capacity-variable way. It is just that this sort of truth proves to be a complex business, with different truths operative at different levels of investigative sophistication. Reality exists all right and has a nature, but the nature of this nature always looks different at the cutting edge.

In the end, the prime lesson to emerge from these considerations is clearly not an indifferentist relativism which says there is no matter-of-fact here, so that you are free to make up your own account in any way you please. Rather it is a *realistic contextualism* whose line is roughly as follows: A given technological state of the art in point of observation and experimentation provides access to a coordinate range of natural phenomena. The resultant data engender the problem of their smooth accommodation by way of theoretical systematization. And this poses an optimization problem of theory-to-data accommodation. Such a problem is one that generally has one or at most a very few optimally effective solutions. And this is certainly not something that we can make up any way we please. Identifying those solutions to problems of theory/data condition is—most emphatically—an objective issue that leaves little if any room for personal inclinations and idiosyncrasies.

And so what we confront in our endeavours to understand nature is to all appearances a reality that is specifically multiplex—rather than merely generically complex—one that presents different aspects of itself at different levels of consideration. The descriptive concepts of physics and the lawful interrelationships that govern them can and to all visible appearances should be seen as artefacts of the interaction between myopia and the level of detail, and the issue of knowledge becomes one of perspective or consideration.[10]

[10] For further ramifications of realism see R. Almeder, *Blind Realism* (Lanham, Md.: Rowman Littlefield, 1992), and N. Rescher, *Scientific Realism* (Dordrecht: Kluwer Academic Publishers, 1987).

4

The Price of an Ultimate Theory

SYNOPSIS

(1) The Principle of Sufficient Reason holds that every fact about the world is explicable on the basis of an explanatory rationale provided by in-principle available theories. (2) The idea of an ultimate theory goes beyond this to insist that one single all-controlling theory can carry the burden. (3) However, this position runs into the problem of how that theory itself is to be explained. (4) The idea of self-explanation has its problems, but a more complex process of co-ordinative systematization offers a more viable option. (5) It is on the basis of the explanatory primacy of system that the idea of an ultimate theory of everything (TOE) is best understood.

4.1. The Principle of Sufficient Reason

The dream of an ultimate theory that explains everything has enchanted philosophers and scientists throughout the centuries. And in the form of an all-encompassing theory of everything—a TOE theory—it continues to beguile physicists in our own day, even long after most professional philosophers have given up on it. A glint in the eyes of many physicists nowadays is the vista of a single overarching 'grand unified theory' that achieves a synoptic explanatory unification of the laws of operation of the fundamental forces at work in physical nature: electromagnetism plus the weak and strong nuclear forces, as well as—ultimately—gravitational force, and perhaps also a somewhat diffuse force of symmetry tropism.[1] Somewhat in

---

[1] See Steven Weinberg, *Dreams of a Final Theory* (New York: Pantheon, 1992), as well as the article 'Grand Unified Theories' by Allan Gut and P. J. Steinhardt in *The Encyclopedia of Cosmology*, ed. N. S. Hetherington (New York: Garland Publishing, 1993), 255–74. See also Edoardo Amaldi, 'The Unity of Physics', *Physics Today*, 261 (Sept. 1973), 23–9. Compare also C. F. von Weizsäcker, 'The Unity of Physics', in Ted Bastin (ed.), *Quantum Theory and Beyond* (Cambridge: Cambridge University Press, 1971).

the manner of a 'superstring' theory that unites all known physical force under the aegis of minuscule stringlike vibrations in space—characterized by Steven Weinberg as 'perhaps the first plausible candidate for a final theory'[2]—it should provide an integrating principle for the fundamental process of physics.

What is at issue here is the ideal of a single, unified principle of explanatory understanding that is at once all-embracingly comprehensive and also final—not in the temporal sense of imperviousness to improvement but rather by way of its comprehensiveness in representing the end of the explanatory line. Such a theory is to constitute the explanatory pivot for all the major questions with which theoretical physics (at least) has to deal. Its task is to provide a grand unified theory able to function as a universal engine for the accomplishment of explanatory work. The pivotal idea is that of securing a key to unlock the cardinal secrets of nature so as to render physical reality comprehensively intelligible.

Considerations of general principle would tend to suggest that this idea of an ultimate scientific theory is bound to encounter large obstacles *en route* to practicable realization. But even before the substantive issues can be addressed profitably, some preliminary clarifications of the theoretical and philosophical background issues are in order.

Confronted with any significant fact, the human mind, by its evolution-imprinted nature, seeks to know the reason why. To all appearances, we stand committed to the idea encapsulated in the classical *principium rationis sufficientis*, the Principle of Sufficient Reason, to the effect that there is always some explanation for why things are as they are, some basis for reaching an understanding of why it is that what is so is so and what is not is not. Let us consider just what it is that this involves.

We shall here use the variables t, t', t'', etc. to range over the set T of factual truths about the physical world.[3] And let us further introduce the abbreviation $t \Sigma t'$ to be construed as t carries the main burden in providing an answer to the explanatory question: 'Why is it that t' obtains?'

---

[2] Weinberg, ibid. 212.

[3] It is questionable, of course, whether it makes sense to contemplate quantifying over truths if we open up the range of fact to the entire spectrum of mathematical potentiality. However, if we limit our purview to the more limited range of facts about the natural world it would seem to become a practicable proposition.

With an explanatory relationship of this general sort in hand, we can delineate the idea of a Principle of Sufficient Reason to the effect that every fact is capable of being explained: that any fact whatsoever can be fitted out with an adequate explanation. In its simplest and most general formulation, such a Principle of Sufficient Reason asserts:

(PSR) $(\forall t)(\exists t')(t' \Sigma t)$

As Leibniz puts it long ago in sect. 32 of the *Monadology* (1716), '[A principle] of sufficient reason [obtains], in virtue of which we consider that no fact could be true or actual, and no proposition true, without there being a sufficient reason for its being so and not otherwise, although most often these reasons cannot be known by us.' This Principle of Sufficient Reason affirms that our questions about the world and its ways always have appropriate answers (however difficult it may prove in practice to come by them). In effect, the principle asserts that:

> For every fact there exists a cogent explanation for its being exactly as it is.

To put it in Hegelian terms, the principle guarantees that the real is rational.

Of course all this still leaves open the matter of just what a satisfactory explanatory answer to a why-question would involve. Science theorists have in recent years devoted much effort to clarifying this issue. But for present purposes we may suppose that it is sufficiently clear to enable people to recognize an acceptable explanation when they see it. As a first approximation we can resort to the familiar Hempelian model of explanation.[4] On this approach, explanation proceeds as follows: If t is a fact to be explained (an *explanandum*) then there will be some more fundamental (that is to say more general and encompassing) fact t' which, in conjunction with some further subsidiary situation-characterizing fact t'' serves as the

[4] The model was initially promulgated in Carl G. Hempel and Paul Oppenheim, 'Studies in Logic of Explanation', *Philosophy of Science*, 15 (1948), 135–75. The historical background of this paper is set out in the author's 'H₂O: Hempel-Helmer-Oppenheim: An Episode in the History of Scientific Philosophy in the Twentieth Century', *Philosophy of Science*, 64 (1997), 779–805; repr. in his *Profitable Speculations* (Lanham, Md.: Rowman Littlefield, 1997), 69–107. The subsequent development of thought about explanation in the middle part of the twentieth century is vividly depicted in Wesley Salmon's *Four Decades of Scientific Explanation* (Minneapolis: University of Minnesota Press, 1990).

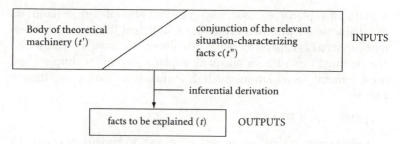

FIG. 4.1 Hempelian explanation

explanatory *explanans* in that it inferentially entails t: $t' \Sigma t$ iff $(\exists t'')[c(t'') \& ([t' \& t''] \to t)]$.[5] Here $\to$ represents inferential derivation and the classifier c indicates that the pertinent fact belongs to the boundary value conditions for the issue under consideration—the conditions that delineate the particular situation at hand in the factual context within which the explanatory problem arises. The resulting picture of explanatory rationalization looks like Fig. 4.1.

The process of explanation here functions in such a way that we would explain *facts* with reference to theories and explain the *theories* themselves, in so far as possible, with reference to other, broader, more high-level theories. Explanatory power cascades downwards to ever lower levels of theoretical generality.

On this basis, the Principle of Sufficient Reason takes the following format:

$$(\forall t)(\exists t')(\exists t'')[c(t'') \& ([t' \& t''] \to t)]$$

In effect, such a Principle of Sufficient Reason holds that with questions about the world's hows and whys we need never in principle confront a situation of total bafflement: whenever matters in the world stand X-wise (for any actual state of affairs whatsoever), then there is a *rationale*—an in-principle discoverable explanation—for why this is so.

With Immanuel Kant, who further elaborated the matter a century after Leibniz, the Principle of Sufficient Reason in its application to this space-time world of ours took the form of a Principle of Causality. This principle asserts that everything that occurs in nature—

---

[5] Hempel-Oppenheim originally said 'deductively' where we have 'inferentially'. Hempel himself later loosened this requirement to contemplate the proposal of probabilistic explanations.

every one of the world's eventuations—has a specifically *causal* explanation: every occurrence is the effect of some cause from which it proceeds under the aegis of the causal laws governing nature's *modus operandi*. Throughout nature, it is efficient causation that always provides for the reason of things. Not only can the world's facts always be explained, but they can always be explained in terms of specifically causal laws.

In the heyday of Newtonian physics this principle was a definitive axiom of scientific philosophy. However, with the rise to prominence of stochastic phenomena in physics and the accompanying emergence of statistical laws, this classically deterministic picture of a world operating under strict causal laws went into decline. The Principle of Causality has vanished in its wake. Probability, chance, and indeterminism come to the fore.

But even though the Kantian Principle of Causality ultimately collapsed, the Principle of Sufficient Reason itself survived this blow. The idea of universal explicability under the aegis of natural laws kept its hold even as these laws changed from a deterministic to a probabilistic character. And in place of the theory of a universally operative causality something rather different emerged.

In replacing the idea of a set of causal laws that can explain anything that occurs in nature, contemporary physics has been drawn to the idea of a comprehensive theory of everything (TOE)—a single complex theory which, even if it cannot explain literally everything, can at any rate explain everything that is explicable. This conception of an ultimate theory has emerged as the modern substitute for the unrealizable old-style Principle of Causality. For while it does not say that everything can be explained on causal principles it says that everything can be explained on TOE-provided principles.

But just exactly what is it that would be required for an 'ultimate' explanatory theory of the sort envisioned by TOE enthusiasts? Somewhat surprisingly, physicists tend not to be very explicit on this critical background issue. Let us take a closer look at it from a philosophical point of view.

4.2. The Idea of an Ultimate Theory

An ultimate theory, of course, is not (or need not be) claimed as chronologically ultimate in the sense of temporal finality—of averting any prospect of change and revision in the wake of scientific progress. It need not be final in the sense of being frozen in time and admitting no further improvement and refinements—of being totally impervious to the prospect of improvement in the light of further information. Rather, the theory must be final in the very different sense of answering all the substantial questions we ask about the *modus operandi* of nature. It must do its synoptic explanatory work but need not be exempt from the prospect of a further development that enables it to do so more effectively and efficiently. Its purported ultimacy is strictly explanatory and thus hermeneutic rather than chronological. But just what does this involve?

To begin with, an ultimate theory must be holistic: it must have the integrity of a collective whole. It cannot be a distributive collective of parts and pieces—a complex aggregate of some sort—but must indeed be a grand unified theory. For we must reject the philosophical doctrine of what has come to be called the Hume–Edwards thesis that:

> If the existence of every member of a set is explained, then the existence of the set is thereby explained.[6]

That this thesis is in fact predicated on a fallacy is not too difficult to see. For consider the following two claims:

- If the existence of every sentence of a paragraph is explained, the existence of that paragraph is thereby explained.
- If the existence of each clause of a contract is explained, the existence of that contract is thereby explained.

Both these claims are clearly false as they stand. On the other hand, contrast these two with the following cognate revisions:

- If the existence of every sentence of a paragraph *as a sentence of that particular paragraph* is explained, then the existence of that paragraph is thereby explained.

---

[6] On this principle in its relation to the cosmological aspect for the existence of God see William L. Rowe, *The Cosmological Argument* (Princeton: Princeton University Press, 1975). See also Richard M. Gale, *On the Nature and Existence of God* (Cambridge: Cambridge University Press, 1991), and Alexander R. Pruss, 'The Hume–Edwards Principle and the Cosmological Argument', *International Journal for Philosophy of Religion*, 434 (1988), 149–65.

- If the existence of every clause of a contract *as a part of that particular contract* is explained, then the existence of that contract is thereby explained.

Both these theses are indeed true—but only subject to that added qualification. After all, to explain the existence of the spouses is not automatically to achieve an explanation of the marital couple, seeing that this would call not just for explaining these participants distributively but their collectively co-ordinated co-presence in the structure at issue. And the case is just the same with the Hume–Edwards thesis. This too is acceptable—but of course only if construed as:

- If the existence of every member of a set *as a member of that particular set* is explained, then the existence of that set is thereby explained.

The fact is that the Hume–Edwards doctrine of distributive explanation is caught on the horns of a dilemma. They can have their pivotal thesis either as it stands or as duly qualified with reference to a required commonality. But in the former case, the thesis is false. And in the latter case it is, though true, unable to bear the reductive burden that its advocates wish to place upon it.[7] For a distributive explanation that is viable will then require a collective explanation of just the sort that those distributionists are seeking to avoid.

The lesson of these deliberations is that that ultimate theory has to be duly holistic. What is needed for a synoptic explanation—and what a TOE theory obviously contemplates—is an unified, integral theory able to achieve the explanatory task on a collective rather than distributive basis. The pathway to an ultimate theory will therefore not be an easy one.

The 'unity of science' to which many theorists aspire may indeed come to be realized at the level of concepts and theories shared between different sciences—that is, at the level of ideational overlaps.

---

[7] In a way, the crux is whether that set is defined extensionally (by way of an inventory) or intensionally (as the set of all items that have the property *P*). In the former case the Hume–Edwards principle holds; in the latter it does not. The existence of each of the things that have *P* may be established without ever mentioning *P*. But if we ask for an explanation of the existence of the set of *P*-possessors then what we want (*inter alia*) is an answer to the generic question of why *P*-possessors exist as such. And of course in asking for an explanation of the existence of 'this particular world', 'this world's things', or 'this world's events/states' (that is of the world's spatiotemporal constituents) we are dealing with something that cannot be inventoried (extensionally specified).

But all available indications are that for every conceptual commonality and shared element there will emerge a dozen differentiations. The increasing complexity of our world picture is a striking phenomenon throughout the development of modern science. Whatever integration may be achieved at the pinnacle of the pyramid will surmount an endlessly expansive range encompassing the most variegated components. It will be an abstract unity that succeeds in uniting a concrete manifold of incredible variety and diversity.

And so the upshot on what is clearly the most direct and natural construction of the ultimacy that a 'theory of everything' is to exhibit, is that two crucial features are principally involved in such an 'ultimate' or 'final' theory—let us designate it by T^*—namely that is internally unified and externally synoptic. Unification, the first of these features, is encapsulated in the principle:

- Explanatory *Comprehensiveness* [C]. Wherever there is a fact, T^* affords its explanation:

$$(\forall t)(T^* \Sigma t)$$

In effect, such explanatory comprehensiveness stipulates T^*'s omnipotence with respect to explanatory questions about the *modus operandi* of nature.

It should be noted that this condition at once entails $(\exists t')(\forall t)(t' \Sigma t)$. And this in turn is something which entails—and is in fact significantly stronger than—the mere Principle of Sufficient Reason: $(\forall t)(\exists t')(t' \Sigma t)$.

The second critical aspect of a TOE-style theory is

- Explanatory *Finality* [F]. There is no further, deeper explanation of T^* itself:

$$\sim (\exists t)(t \Sigma T^* \,\&\, t \neq T^*) \text{ or equivalently } (\forall t)(t \Sigma T^* \to t = T^*)$$

This means that the possibilities are reduced to the point where the only conceivably appropriate explanation of T^* is T^* itself. With the possible exception of T^* itself, nothing else is available that is in a position to provide an explanation of T^*: it stands at the end of the explanatory line.

The availability of a comprehensive and final explanatory theory along these lines—one that is capable of accounting for the laws of nature themselves—constitutes the core of the doctrine of grand unified explicability. As the very name suggests, unity and comprehensiveness must characterize any such grand unified theory.[8]

4.3. An Aporetic Situation

Now the crucial consideration for present purposes is that the idea of an ultimate theory along the indicated lines stands in decided conflict with a principle that lies at the heart of the traditional conception of explanatory adequacy, namely a stipulation to the following effect:

- *Explanatory Non-circularity* [N]. No satisfactory explanation can invoke the very fact that is itself to be explained. No fact explains itself.

$$\sim (\exists t)(t\Sigma t)$$

This clearly fundamental non-circularity principle obtains because it is obviously problematic to deploy a theory for its own explanation. No blatantly circular explanation can ever be altogether satisfactory, seeing that it presumes the explanatory availability of the very item whose explanation is at issue.

And just here is the point where trouble ensues for any sort of ultimate theory. For observe that Comprehensiveness at once entails $T^*\Sigma T^*$. And, moreover, there is another route to the same destination even without proceeding via comprehensiveness:

1. $(\exists t)t\Sigma T^*$ by PSR
2. $T^*\Sigma T^*$ from 1 by Finality

Both of these pathways lead us to a conflict with Non-circularity, so that both Comprehensiveness and Finality are in trouble as long as Non-circularity is maintained.

Diagramatically we have the situation with respect to implication relationships as shown in Fig. 4.2.

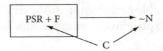

FIG. 4.2 Deductive relations between explanatory principles

[8] See Steven Weinberg, *Dreams of a Final Theory* (New York: Pantheon, 1992).

What this means is that in espousing *N* one must abandon *C* and (if one wishes to retain *PSR*) also *F* as well. And so a TOE theorist committed to *C* and *F* is bound to regard the non-circularity principle *N* as something that has to be jettisoned.

But non-circularity is not so easily abandoned. For what we now have is the distinctly problematic idea of circular self-explanation at exactly the most crucial juncture of our explanatory project. The unhappy precedent of *causa sui* theorizing in theology looms before us here. This problematic option exacts what is, to all appearances, an altogether unacceptable price.

The fatal flaw of any purported explanatory theory of everything arises in connection with the ancient paradox of reflectivity and self-substantiation. How can any theory adequately substantiate itself? *Quis custodiet ipsos custodes?* What are we to make of the individual—or the doctrine—that claims, 'I stand ready to vouch for myself'? And how can such self-substantiation possibly be made effective? All the old difficulties of reflexivity and self-reference come to the fore here.[9] No painter can paint a comprehensive picture of a setting that includes this picture itself. And no more, it would seem, can a theorist propound an explanatory account of nature that claims to account satisfactorily for that account itself. For in so far as that account draws on itself, this very circumstance undermines its viability.

The upshot of such considerations is that an adequate ultimate theory of scientific explanation, naïvely understood as satisfying all of the traditional explanatory desiderata, is in principle impossible.

And the reason for this state of affairs is easily grasped. For consider again:

(PSR)   Every fact has a satisfactory explanation.

(N)   Nothing is self-explanatory: a satisfying explanation must always lie in something yet deeper.

These principles launch us into an explanatory regress that looks to the prospect of progressively deepening our explanation. And this seemingly indispensable escape-route from vitiating regress is cut off by supposing the explanatively ultimate cul-de-sac of an ultimate explanation.

---

[9] See T. S. Champlain, *Reflexive Paradoxes* (London: Routledge, 1988), and S. J. Bartlett and P. Suber (eds.), *Self-Reference* (Dordrecht: Martinus Nijhoff, 1987). See also Thomas Breuer, 'Universal und unvollständig: Theorien über alles?', *Philosophia Naturalis*, 34 (1997), 1–20.

4.4. A Way Out of the Impasse

How can one find an exit from this labyrinth?

The most promising way out of the impasse seems to lie in returning to square one and taking another look at the very idea of explanation itself. And this being so, a TOE theorist is well advised to go back to the drawing-board and reconsider the naïve theory of explanatory adequacy.

As noted above, contemporary explanation theory generally construes this on the lines of the deductive model urged in the classic pages of Hempel and Oppenheim. Recall the tenor of the Hempelian position regarding the *modus operandi* of explanation, which can be represented as in Fig. 4.3.

Given this understanding of the matter, explanation clearly becomes something that has to move from the more basic to the derivative. On Hempelian principles, the explanatory process continues to implement Aristotle's idea of substantive priority that sees the explanans as more fundamental and far-reaching than the explanandum. Explanation stands committed to unidirectional priority.

And on this basis there would be no reason to countenance the prospect of an ultimate theory. As Karl Popper put it, in rejecting 'the idea of an ultimate explanation' we must acknowledge that 'every explanation may be further explained by a theory or conjecture of a higher degree of universality. There can be no explanation which is not in need of a further explanation.'[10]

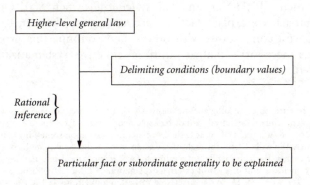

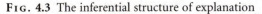

FIG. 4.3 The inferential structure of explanation

[10] K. R. Popper, *Objective Knowledge: An Evolutionary Approach* (Oxford: Clarendon Press, 1972), 195.

But this idea of an endless generality regress in explanation is deeply problematic. In a universe based on the operation of fundamental forces that are, presumably, finite in number, it would indeed seem that an explanatory regress will have to terminate in some altogether unexplained explainer. We seem to be driven to something that is supposed to be explanatorily fundamental and yet itself altogether unexplained.[11]

There is, however, a promising alternative here—a very different way of understanding how explanation can work. For instead of giving our explanations through an inferential subsumption under prior, more fundamental theses, one can take resort to a variant mode of explanation—one that proceeds not via prior premisses but via posterior consequences. Such an essentially teleological approach offers the option of explaining a fact through the consideration that it itself serves to account for a significant spectrum of other things. On this basis our explanations proceed not by derivation from prior basics but through the fertility of results—and thus through their systemic role in the overall fabric of inferential systematization. In taking such a pragmatic point of view we are led to a dualized conception of explanation as a process that can proceed either by way of direct *derivation* (as per →) or by way of the *systematization* (**S**) that is achieved when t is inferentially embedded in the wider setting of an overall system of explanatory understanding. In thus going to a two-tier mode of explanation, we envision two different ways of 'explaining' a thesis t: (1) *inferentially* when $(\exists t')(t' \Sigma t)$, and (2) *systemically* when $S(t)$. On such an approach we explain facts by accounting for them in terms of their lawful connections with others, and continue this process as long as necessary—that is, until a cohesive systematization is achieved.

---

[11] To be sure, some theologians incline to say that there are ultimate facts about the world which, while they indeed cannot be explained by other facts about the world, are nevertheless not unexplained because their explanation rests upon something extramundane, namely the will of God through his decision to have those ultimate facts about the world be as they are. Thus, while those ultimate facts are not world-internally explainable, they nevertheless admit of a world-external explanation. (Cf. J. Polkinghorne, *Science and Creation: The Search for Understanding* (New York: Random House, 1988); *God's Action in the World* (Berkeley: Center of Theology and Natural Science Public Forums, 1990).) The difficulty here is that if the will of God is not to be arbitrary, irrational, and despotic (*stat pro ratione voluntas*), there must be some *reason* for God's decision, and since it is a decision *about the world* it must have a basis in some feature of the world itself.

But how are we to explain the laws of nature themselves (or *purported* laws of nature, strictly speaking)? Will law explanations not always leave something unaccounted for?

In general, laws are explained by their derivation from other laws. This is clearly a process that must come to a stop. The set of laws of nature—as best we can develop it—is always finite. With facts we can in principle go on ad infinitum in referring them to others, but with laws this process must have a stop: the subsumptive explanation of laws must eventually come to the end of the road. Here we will always reach certain ultimate, axiomatic principles. How, then, do we explain these?

Do we not at this stage reach a limit of sorts? If the ultimate or fundamental laws play the role of basic premises in science, much as the axioms are basic in a system of geometry, does this not render them inexplicable? For although science uses them in giving explanations, they will themselves lie outside the range of scientific explicability.

The answer here lies in recognizing that the axioms of our law systems are not inexplicable ultimates. For one thing, their being axiomatic is largely incidental. Axioms, after all, are axioms not because of what they say but because of how we fit them into the organization of our knowledge. Axiomaticity is a matter of the particular systematization of information we find it advantageous to adopt. (What is axiomatic in one system might well be theorematic in another.) But be this as it may, the critical fact is that axioms too are explicable. Not, however, through derivation from other, still more fundamental theses—which would, after all, make these the true axioms, and the original ones mere pretenders. Rather, axioms find their explanation systemically, in terms of their role in that whole system—as being needed to give rise to the whole elegantly and efficiently. Even so must 'ultimate' laws be accounted for in terms of their integrative role in the entire law system.

The traditional subsumptive approach thus stands in contrast to a very different one that proceeds non-subsumptively on the basis of 'best-fit' considerations. The best fit ('coordination') at issue may involve *inferential connectedness*, but it may also be a matter of analogy, uniformity, simplicity, and the other facets of systematization. Thus, we have here a wholly different approach to explanation; one that takes systematization itself as the key, relying not on subsumptive inference but on systemic coordination. Here the issue is not subordination to, but coordination with: it is not a matter of inference from other theses at all but one of optimal meshing through mutual attunement with them. On such an approach, if we explain A with reference to B and C, we do so not by inferring A from B and C but by showing that A is more smoothly co-systematizable with B and C than is the case with any of its plausible alternatives, A', A'', and so on.

The idea of an explanatory bedrock—of certain ultimate, altogether axiomatic, and inexplicable theses that simply do not need explanation—is not very satisfying and is, moreover, quite unnecessary. The sensible view is simply that different modes of explanation are at issue at different levels of discussion. In endowing the theories of science with an axiomatic development, we 'explain' the theorems *subsumptively* because the axioms yield them, but we explain the axioms *co-ordinatively* because they engender the appropriate theorems and provide for the right systemic results. The law-axioms are explained teleologically, as it were, because the processes they represent must obtain in order for the system to function efficiently and effectively. The 'ultimate laws' are explained through their capacity to underwrite the holistic integrity of the entire system.

Accordingly, axioms are *not* inherently inexplicable. Systemic unity serves as the overarching principle of explanatory legitimation in providing the framework through which axioms themselves are accounted.[12]

In the wake of this enlarged understanding of explanation we must now change the specific nature of Comprehensiveness from $(\forall t)[T^*\Sigma t]$ to:

$$(C') \quad (\forall t)[T^*\Sigma t \vee S(t)].$$

And moreover, we correspondingly change the Principle of Sufficient Reason (PSR) from $(\forall t)(\exists t')(t'\Sigma t)$ to

$$(\text{PSR}') \quad (\forall t)[(\exists t')(t'\Sigma t) \vee S(t)].$$

And it is now clear that these revised versions of C' and PSR$'$ are perfectly compatible with Finality (F) and Non-circularity (N).

The aporetic inconsistency that initially confronted us is now avoided: there is no longer any sort of conflict among our various

---

[12] Compare the author's *Cognitive Systematization* (Oxford: Basil Blackwell, 1980) for a fuller development of these ideas.

fundamental theses. The revised principles conspire in indicating that in the particular case of T^*, at least, the proper mode of explanation lies in the S-mode, so that we have $S(T^*)$. In taking recourse to the second mode of systemic explanation represented by S and readjusting our theses in its light we thus restore peace and harmony in the family of explanatory principles.[13]

Moreover, other considerations also support this change in the construction of PSR. For as long as we interpret this principle with 'explanation' understood in a subsumptive (Hempelian) manner we cannot avert the Hobson's choice between circular explanation, infinite regress, or inherent necessity—as Aristotle has already indicated in his *Posterior Analytics*. So the recourse to explanatory systematicity seems to be desirable in any case.

But how is the sort of systematization at issue here to be understood: how does S work? Specifically, what will systematization look like at the level of an ultimate theory T^* at the cosmological level? To address this issue, consider the three basic elements of our account

$T^* = $ the grand ultimate theory itself

$T = t_1 \& t_2 \& \ldots \& t_n = $ the conjunction of our various detailed theories of physical explanation.

$B = b_1 \& b_2 \& \ldots \& b_n = $ the conjunction of the basic observed and calculated boundary value conditions for physical explanation—including, in particular, the fundamental constants of nature.

Now in looking to systematization in this context we would, presumably, have three desiderata in view:

1. $T^* + B$ explains T—and does so in something like the Hempelian subsumptive manner. The conjoining of T^* with the various boundary-value conditions should provide a suitable (subsumptive) explanation of principal physical theories themselves.

2. $T + B$ substantiates T^*. T^* should be an optimal solution to the question: Given B and T, what sort of unified higher-level account provides for the optimal systemic unification of the components of T?

---

[13] Observe that if we were to proceed on analogy with the above to change N to: (N′) $\sim (\exists t)[\sim S(t) \& t\Sigma t]'$ or equivalently $(\forall t)(t\Sigma t \supset S(t))]$ then we can tolerate the idea of self-explanation in the special case of $T^*\Sigma T^*$ because this would only imply that $S(T^*)$, which we accept. And of course with *mundane* facts—where T^* certainly is not—we can continue to insist upon precluding self-explanation.

3. $T^* + T$ determines B. In so far as possible, the purely theoretical considerations of T^* and T should constrain the fundamental constants of nature and the world's fundamental boundary-value conditions. But where such categorical value-constraint is unachievable, it should at least transpire that the theoretical resources render their actually observed values maximally probable, so that, operating in the manner of the Anthropic Principle, they render the determinable boundary-value conditions of the existing order of nature maxiprobable in relation to possible alternatives. The characteristic features of the world as we have it should be probabilized by the laws of nature that we accept.

In this way we have the situation that the trio T^*, T, and B is so interdependently connected in its cognitive interrelationship that, given any two of its members, the third becomes fixed in place. This sort of integrating interconnection is, clearly, the optimal way of providing for the systematic integration of our ultimate theory T^*. Systemic coherence here provides the explanatory pivot within the wider framework of our physical knowledge. And it would, ideally, be in its capacity to play this integrative role that the systemic 'explanation' of our ultimate theory consists.[14]

4.5. Implications

These considerations put us into a position to deal with the holistic question of why the overall framework of scientific fact and law and system should be as it is. The question is, if explanation at the level of facts and laws is inevitably intra-systemic, what is to explain the whole system itself?

In a way, this question is an invitation to folly. We clearly cannot provide a scientific explanation for the whole system of science in terms of something that falls outside: it would not be the whole system if anything fell outside it. Explanatory self-subsumption is infeasible at the level of facts and laws. But at the systemic level it is a conditional necessity: if the system can be explained at all, that explanation must fall within it. As long as we operate on scientific principles, we cannot get outside the framework of our completed

---

[14] The author's *Limits of Science*, rev. edn. (Pittsburgh: University of Pittsburgh Press, 1999), deals with further issues relevant to this discussion.

explanatory system: to explain the system in terms of *X* would simply be to enlarge it to include *X* itself. The quest for a system-external foundation for the scientific rationalization of the system is ultimately senseless. We explain facts in terms of other facts and laws. We explain laws in terms of facts, laws, and systemic principles. And we explain systems self-referentially in terms of the laws they are able to systematize. The laws that comprise the system must have a substantive content that accommodates certain crucial structural systemic principles (for example, universality, economy, homogeneity) paramount, principles which, in their turn, serve to account for the character of those laws themselves. The laws, that is, are explained through the fact that constitute a law-system optimally designed in line with these features will have exactly the character of the laws at issue.[15]

The resultant situation is indeed cyclical and perhaps even circular. But this simply reflects the structural coherence of rational systematization. Facts are explained from above, via the laws they instantiate; systems from below, via the laws they rationalize. Laws can be approached from either end—via the facts they coordinate or via the family of laws with which they stand in systemic coordination. The overall process is not a vicious but a virtuous circle of self-substantiation. Adequacy lies not in a unidirectional flow from the more basic to the less so but in the smooth meshing of the overall cycle of interrelationships.[16]

The principles of systematization consequently have the feature that they are themselves monitored by an overarching structure of systemic order. This closing of the cycle of substantiation is itself an aspect of systematicity. The adequacy of our explanatory systematizing is thus itself controlled by systematic considerations. In the final analysis, then, we explain the system-as-a-whole through its capacity efficiently to do the job of scientific rationalization. This, however, is not a defect of our explanatory capacities but an immediate and inevitable consequence of the nature of an explanatory system.

---

[15] An analogy may help: that of the poet who in composing an *Arspoetica* poem to formulate his principles of prosody also manages to present a paradigmatic illustration of them.

[16] Compare the author's *Methodological Pragmatism* (Oxford: Basil Blackwell, 1973).

The issue of legitimation is thus settled in terms of a cyclic inter-dependence and self-supportiveness. The idea of explanatory strat-ification is misleading: no neat linear order of fundamentality obtains among nature's facts of laws. No useful work can be done for us by the Aristotelian principle that explanation must always and every-where proceed unidirectionally from what is more fundamental or basic to what is less so. The ancient search for linear priority in matters of scientific explanation can be carried only so far.

And so we can return to the issue posed by our initial question of the cost of an ultimate theory. This, so it now emerges, is that we must modify—and complicate—the generally accepted view of the nature of explanation itself[17] by taking a two-track approach to explanation either via antecedents or alternatively via consequences. Over and above the prospect of explanation by inference from more fundamental priors we must resort to the idea of 'explaining' a theory in terms of its posterior consequences—that is, in terms of what goes after rather than what come before. We must be prepared on occasion to resolve our explanatory questions by non-standard means and to adopt—at lease in some cases—a *coherence theory* of explanation. For in at least one case—that of the ultimate theory itself—we must explain matters in the same—and indeed the only—way in which we can explain the axioms of a formalized theory: not by derivation from something yet more fundamental, but by taking note of the circumstance that it represents a commitment that leads to the right sorts of consequential results.

In theory, to be sure, we need resort to this complication of dualized explanation only in the case of the ultimate theory itself. There is, however, no need to be quite that squeamish about this useful device. For what now clearly emerges is that in *some* cases, at any rate, it deserves to be seen as natural and appropriate to take such a perspectively oriented approach. And this is something which is in principle capable of extension across a wider range.

The fact of the matter is that such a complication in our concept of explanation brings with it some not insignificant theoretical advant-ages. For what we now have is, in effect, a dualizing of explanatory dimensions. An explanation can now be extended in two different

---

[17] A discussion which reaches much the same doctrinal destination by a very different route—one that proceeds via predominantly historical rather than logico-theoretical con-siderations—is Philip Kitcher's 'Explanatory Unification', *Philosophy of Science*, 48 (1981), 507–31.

ways. Either in *depth*, by furthering the regressive search for reasons why behind the reasons why, or in *breadth*, by extending the patterns of systemic coherence through which we amplify the systemic enmeshment of the item to be explained into the wider framework of our relevant commitments. What is lost in simplicity in dualizing our concept of explanation is more than compensated for by what we gain in range and power.

Viewed as a theoretical desideratum, an ultimate theory is to be a unified explanatory principle that dispenses with a disaggregated proliferation of explanatory devices. It enables us to discharge the explanatory mission of physical science on a unitized and collective rather than a fragmented and distributive basis. However, as the preceding deliberations indicate, the question of how such a final theory itself is to be explained cannot be avoided. And it is here that a compensatory price is exacted from us. For we have no alternative but to see the explanation of an ultimate theory to lie in the diversified justification of explanatory work that it facilitates. And at this point diversity and plurality forces its way to the forefront again. For the explanatory justification of the theory itself is something that is achieved only distributively on the basis of that complex array of explanatory tasks that the theory is able to accomplish. On the revised explanatory perspective that is now at issue, it is the very considerations that qualify a theory to be considered as a 'grand unified theory' that themselves now serve to explain that theory and thereby to provide its legitimative substantiation.

If ultimate questions are to be resolved satisfactorily, what is needed is not so much an ultimate *answer* as an ultimate *process* for the provision of answers, a process for which a complexity-embracing cognitive systematization provides the cornerstone. And on this basis the explanation of our explanatorily ultimate or final theory itself lies in the very fact of its being able to accomplish effectively and efficiently the synoptic explanatory task for which it is designed. The price of an ultimate theory, then, is thoroughgoing systematization—albeit of a sort that is bound to grow increasingly more complex and internally diversified with the progress of natural sciences.

5

Ramifications of Realism

SYNOPSIS

(1) Scientific realism—the doctrine that science correctly describes the real world—is in this form unrealistic in view of science's ongoing change of mind about how the world works. All that can be said is that science aims at describing reality correctly. (2) Physical realism, by contrast, is the less ambitious doctrine that the objects of physics are actually real and not mere figments of our speculation—imperfect though our understanding of them may be. What is perhaps the strongest argument for such realism is the very imperfection of our knowledge, whose course of development constantly brings home to us the lesson that nature is vastly more complex than ever imagined. (3) Finally, metaphysical realism maintains the existence of a mind-independent, natural reality about which we can secure at least some objectively descriptive information (however incomplete and imperfect). (4) Such a position is a presuppositional commitment for the project of scientific inquiry rather than a discovered product of its operation. And its justification lies largely in considerations of utility in both theoretical and practical regards.

5.1. Problems of Scientific Realism

The American philosopher Brand Blanshard told the story of how his Oxford tutor H. H. Joachim once asked him during an afternoon walk, 'Do you suppose that there really *are* such things as atoms?'[1] Prior to World War I, this may have seemed a genuinely problematic issue. But in due course, and after Hiroshima especially, it ceased to seem plausible to question the existence of atomic particles. To all

---

[1] P. A. Schilpp (ed.), *The Philosophy of Brand Blanshard* (La Salle, Ill.: Open Court, 1980), 20.

appearances, the progress of science and technology transformed the situation.

Philosophical realism as a general doctrine maintains that there is a domain of mind-independent existence and that we can obtain *some* reliable knowledge of it. But where are we to look for such reality-characterizing knowledge? The most attractive and plausible line of response here is that natural science is our best route to information about objective reality. This, at any rate, is the pivotal idea of the doctrine of scientific realism. And so, the exponents of this position hold that natural science affords accurate and reliable information about reality, maintaining that if we want to know about the kinds of things there are in the world and the sorts of properties they have, then it is to science that we should turn.

Such a position reaches well beyond a generalized metaphysical realism that goes no further than maintaining that there is a mind-independent reality and that we can know *something* about it. For scientific realism moves on to say (1) that we can come to know a great deal about it; (2) that this knowledge relates not just to peripheral matters but to essentials; and (3) that this information is provided through science. Natural science—so it maintains—gives an appropriate account of the salient and characteristic features of what objectively exists in the real (mind-independent) world. Its theories regarding non-observable entities—subatomic particles, electromagnetic fields, gravitational space-warps, and the rest—characterize the actual properties of real things in the real world, things every bit as real as the animals and plants and rocks that we see with our own eyes.

Scientific realism in its most ambitious version, then, is the doctrine that science describes the real world—that the world actually is pretty much as science takes it to be and that its furnishings are pretty much as science envisions them to be.[2] It maintains that such theoretical entities as the quarks and electrons of contemporary subatomic physics are perfectly real components of nature's 'real world,' every bit as real as acorns and grains of sand. The latter we observe with the naked eye, the former we detect by complex theoretical triangulation. But a scientific realism of theoretical entities maintains that this difference is incidental. On such a realistic construction of

[2] Ontological realism contrasts with ontological idealism; while scientific realism contrasts with scientific instrumentalism: the doctrine that science in no way *describes* reality, but merely affords a useful organon of prediction and control.

scientific theorizing, the declarations of science are factually true generalizations about the actual behaviour of real physical objects existing in nature. Those unobservable entities exist in just the way in which the scientific theories that project them maintain. The core of scientific realism is inherent in its equating the theory-creatures envisioned in natural science with the domain of what actually exists.

But this ambitious equation would work only if our science, as it stands here and now—the only science we ever actually have—really has it right. This is something we are certainly not able—and not entitled—to maintain. For the theoretical entities envisioned by current frontier science will only exist just as current science envisions them in so far as current frontier science is in fact correct—only if it manages to get things just right. And this view that current science has it altogether right evidently has its problems. For science constantly changes its mind, not just with regard to incidentals but even on very fundamental issues. The history of science is the story of the replacement of one inadequate theory by yet another that sees its predecessors as enmeshed in misleading oversimplifications. So how can one plausibly maintain a scientific realism geared to the idea that 'science as we now have it at the cutting-edge frontier correctly describes reality'?

Natural science consistently changes its mind. There is virtually nothing about which the science of today thinks in exactly the same way as the science of a generation—let alone a century—ago.

If the past betokens the future—if historical experience affords any sort of guidance in these matters—then we can confidently expect the presently favoured theses and theories of frontier science will ultimately turn out to be untenable in their present form—that none are correct exactly as is. All the experience we can muster indicates that there is no justification for viewing our science as more than an inherently imperfect stage within an ongoing development. The ineliminable prospect of far-reaching future changes of mind in scientific matters destroys any prospect of claiming that the world is as we now claim it to be—that science's view of nature's constituents and laws is correct.

The ultimate untenability of current scientific theories is in fact one of the very few points of consensus of modern philosophy. When Karl Popper insists that from a rational point of view, 'we should not "rely" on any (scientific) theory, for no theory has been shown to be true, or can be shown to be true',[3] he speaks for the entire tradition of modern science scholarship from Charles Sanders Peirce to Nancy Cartwright. We must unhesitatingly presume that, as we manage to push our inquiries through to deeper levels of understanding, we will get a very different view of the constituents of nature and their *modus operandi*. Its changeability in the wake of progress is a fact *about* science that is as inductively well-established as any theory *of* science itself. Science is not a static system but a dynamic process.

All too clearly, then, there is insufficient warrant for and little plausibility to the claim that the world is as our present-day science claims it to be—that our science is correct science and offers the definitive last word on the issues regarding its creatures-of-theory. We can learn by empirical inquiry about empirical inquiry itself. And one of the key things to be learnt is that at no actual stage does natural science yield a firm, final, unchanging result. The current state of scientific frontier knowledge is simply one among others that share the same imperfect footing as regards ultimate correctness or definitive truth. No matter what the calendar says, we must realize there is a strong prospect that we shall ultimately recognize many or most of our current scientific theories to be false and that what we proudly vaunt as scientific knowledge is a tissue of hypotheses—of tentatively adopted contentions many or most of which we will ultimately come to regard needing serious revision or perhaps even abandonment.

This state of affairs clearly blocks the option of scientific realism of any straightforward sort. Not only are we not in a position to claim that our knowledge of reality is *complete* (that we have gotten at the *whole* truth of things), but we are not even in a position to claim that our knowledge of reality is *correct* (that we have discovered the real truth of things). Such a position calls for the humbling view that just as we think our predecessors of a hundred years ago had a fundamentally inadequate grasp on the ways of the world, so our successors of a hundred years hence will take the same view of our purported knowledge of things.

We have to come to terms with the realism-impending fact that our scientific knowledge of the world fails in crucial respects to give an accurate picture of it. At the level of its technical theories science is

---

[3] Karl R. Popper, *Objective Knowledge: An Evolutionary Approach* (Oxford: Clarendon Press, 1972), 9.

a matter not of truth provision but of truth estimation. We subscribe for the most part to the working hypothesis that in the domain of factual inquiry *our* truth may be taken to be *the* truth. All the same, we realize full well that our science is not definitive, that reality is not actually as we currently picture it to be, that our truth is not the real truth, that we are probably quite wrong in supposing that the objects 'our science' purports to address actually exist exactly as it conceives them to be. No doubt reality itself, whatever that may be, stands secure, but our empirical reality—reality exactly as our science expects it here and now—is a fiction. Our scientific description of reality is a mind-devised, man-made artefact that cannot actually be accepted at face value. Ultimately, when science is seen in its historical perspectives as the ongoing process it is, it becomes clear that there is no adequate justification for thinking that natural science as we now have it is definitively correct.

Postulating the reality of science's commitments is thus viable only if done provisionally, in the spirit of doing the best we can manage at present, in the current state of the art. Our prized scientific knowledge is no more than our current best estimate of the matter. The step of reification is always to be taken provisionally, subject to a mental reservation of presumptive revisability.

A clear distinction must accordingly be maintained between our scientific conception of reality and reality as it really is. We realize that there is precious little justification for holding that the thesis of natural science at the frontier of current research actually describes reality and depicts the world as it really is. And this constitutes a decisive impediment to any straightforward realism. It must inevitably constrain and condition our attitude towards the natural mechanisms envisioned in contemporary science. We certainly do not—or should not—want to reify (hypostatize) the theoretical entities of current frontier science, to say flatly and without qualification that the contrivances of *our* present-day science correctly depict the furniture of the real world. We do not—or at any rate, given the realities of the case, should not—want to adopt categorically the ontological implications of scientific theorizing in just exactly the state-of-the-art configuration presently in hand. A realistic acknowledgment of scientific fallibilism precludes the claim that the furnishings of the real world are exactly as our science states them to be—that electrons actually are just what the latest *Handbook of Physics* claims them to be. We can be fairly confident that the science of the future will amplify and correct that of our day—though we are not, of course, in a position to say just where and how. No frontier thesis of current science stands secure. Accordingly, only a modest version of scientific realism is in order—one that envisions as no more than loose coupling between the nature of reality and the science of the day— the only science that we have.

Perhaps, however, a more millenarian sort of realism can be maintained—one that looks to science of the future. Despite our science's failure to characterize the real adequately, perhaps that of our successors will do so. Though this view is worth contemplating, its prospects are not auspicious. For the question arises, just which future? After all, there is little reason to think that the status of tomorrow's science is in principle different from that of today's. It seems to be the inevitable destiny of physics that its practitioners in every generation will see the theories of an earlier era as mistaken, as full of errors of omission and commission as well. In determinable likelihood the physicists in the year 3000 will deem our physics no more correct than we deem that of a hundred years ago—and the same destiny of ultimate revision awaits their own views in turn. The reality, as best we can tell, is that the equilibrium achieved by physical science at *any* given stage of its development is always an unstable one. Its theories have a finite lifespan. Only the aims of natural science are stable, not its substantive questions—let alone its answers to them.

The idea of definitively correct science is no more (though also no less) than an idealization, representing an ideal which, like other ideals, is worthy of pursuit, despite the fact that we must recognize that its full attainment lies beyond our grasp. A doctrinal scientific realism is thus flawed because we cannot say decisively that science describes reality. What we can say—and all that we can say—is that (1) science *aims* at giving us a cognitively useful model of reality, and (2) the science of the day provides us with the best description of reality that we currently have—the best *estimate* that is available to us. Only such a cautious scientific realism—a rather modest and watered-down version of the doctrine—merits endorsement.[4]

This cautious perspective does not deconstruct the idea of scientific knowledge; for recall that we are here talking about knowledge at

---

[4] Some further considerations relevant to this chapter's deliberations are elaborated in N. Rescher, *Empirical Inquiry* (Totowa, NJ: Rowman & Littlefield, 1982), and *Scientific Realism* (Dordrecht: D. Reidel, 1987).

the cutting edge frontier of present-day science. Now with regard to the science of the day, S_t *with* $t = n$ for 'now'—we ourselves un- questionably are tempted to endorse the inference schema: If $p \in S$, then p. At the level of specific claims, we have little alternative but to look upon *our* knowledge as real knowledge—a thesis p would not be part of *our* truth if we did not take it to form part of *the* truth. The answers we give to our questions are literally the best we can provide. The knowledge at issue is to be knowledge according to our own lights—the only ones we have. But despite our resort to this adequacy principle at the level of particular claims, we nevertheless acknow- ledge the need to abjure the hubris of claiming that our science has it right.

The relationship of our (putative) scientific knowledge to the (real) truth has to be conceived of in terms of estimation. At the frontiers of generality and precision, 'our truth' in matters of scient- ific theorizing is not—and may well never actually be—the real truth. Science does not *secure* the truth (deliver it into our hands in its definitive finality). We have no alternative to acknowledging that our science, as it stands here and now, does not present the real but provides us with a tentative and provisional *estimate* of it. However confidently it may affirm its conclusions, the realization must be maintained that the declarations of natural science are provisional and tentative—subject to revision and even to outright rejection. The most we can ever do is to take our science (S_n) as the imperfect best we can do here and now to conjecture the real truth.

It is certain that there is no question that we can improve our science. The history of science cries out for the Whig interpretation. Every applicable standard, from systemic sophistication to practical applicability, yields reason to think that later science is better science. But of course this does not mean that later science is any the *truer*— for true it cannot be if it, too, is destined for eventual rejection. The standards of scientific acceptability do not and cannot assure actual or indeed even probable or approximate truth. As Larry Laudan has argued with substantial evidence and eloquence, 'No one has been able even to say what it would mean to be "closer to the truth", let alone to offer criteria for determining how we could assess such proximity.'[5] All claims that emerge from scientific theorizing are

---

[5] Larry Laudan, as cited in Ilkka Niiniluoto, 'Scientific Progress', *Synthese*, 45 (1980), 446. Rejection of the idea that science gets at the truth of things goes back to Karl Popper.

vulnerable—subject to improvement and replacement. We can claim that later, 'superior' science affords a better warranted estimate of the truth, but we cannot claim that it manages somehow to capture more of the truth or to approximate to it more closely.[6]

Interestingly enough, in point of vulnerability science compares unfavourably with the commonplace knowledge of matters of pre-scientific fact—our knowledge regarding sticks and stones and sealing wax and the other paraphernalia of everyday life. And there is good reason for this.

Increased security can always be purchased for our estimates at the price of decreased accuracy. We estimate the height of a tree at around 25 feet. We are quite sure that the tree is 25 ± 5 feet high. We are virtually certain that its height is 25 ± 10 feet. But we are completely and absolutely sure that its height is between 1 inch and 100 yards. Of this we are completely sure in the sense that we are absolutely certain, certain beyond the shadow of a doubt, as certain as we can be of anything in the world, so sure that we would be willing to stake our life on it, and the like. For any sort of estimate whatso-ever, there is always a characteristic trade-off between the evidential security or reliability of the estimate, on the one hand (as determin-able on the basis of its probability or degree of acceptability), and, on the other hand, its contentual *definiteness* (exactness, detail, preci-sion, etc.). A situation of the sort depicted by the concave curve of Fig. 5.1 obtains.

Now, the crucial point is that natural science eschews the security of indefiniteness. In science we operate at the right-hand side of the diagram: we always strive for the maximal achievable universality,

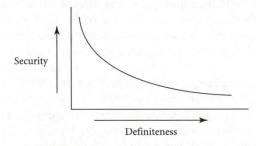

FIG. 5.1 The degradation of security with increasing definiteness

[6] See the author's *Induction* (Oxford: Blackwell, 1980).

precision, exactness, and so on. The law-claims of science are *strict*: precise, wholly explicit, exceptionless, and unshaded. They involve no hedging, no fuzziness, no incompleteness, and no exceptions. In stating that the melting point of lead is 327.545°C at standard pressure, the physicist asserts that all pieces of (pure) lead will unfailingly melt at this temperature; he certainly does not mean to assert that most pieces of (pure) lead will probably melt at somewhere around this temperature. By contrast, when we assert in ordinary life that peaches are delicious, we mean something like, 'most people will find the eating of suitably grown and duly matured peaches a relatively pleasurable experience'. Such statements have all sorts of built-in safeguards, such as 'more or less,' 'in ordinary circumstances', 'by and large', 'normally', 'if other things are equal', and so on. They are not laws but rules of thumb, a matter of practical lore rather than scientific rigour. In natural science, however, we deliberately accept risk by aiming at maximal definiteness—and thus at maximal informativeness and testability. The theories of natural science take no notice of what happens ordinarily or normally; they seek to transact their explanatory business in terms of high generality and strict universality—in terms of what happens always and everywhere and in all circumstances. In consequence, we must recognize the vulnerability of our scientific statements. The fact that the theoretical claims of science are mere estimates that are always cognitively at risk and enjoy only a modest lifespan has its roots in science's inherent commitment to the pursuit of maximal definiteness. Its cultivation of informativeness (of definiteness of information) everywhere forces science to risk error.

A tenable fallibilism must take this inverse relationship between definiteness and security into careful account. Consider the Atomic Theory, for example. It has an ancient and distinguished history in the annals of science, stretching from the speculations of Democritus in antiquity, through the work of Dalton, Rutherford, and Bohr, to the baroque complexities of the present day. 'It is surely unlikely that science will ever give up on atoms!' you say. Quite true! But what we are dealing with here is clearly not *a* scientific theory at all, but a vast family of scientific theories, a great bundle loosely held together by threads of historical influence and family resemblances. There is not much that Rutherford's atoms, and Bohr's, and those of our contemporary quantum theorists have in common. As such, the Atomic Theory is no more than a rough generic schema based on the more or less metaphorical intuition that 'matter is granular in the small, composed of tiny structures separated in space'. This is surely incomplete and indeterminate—a large box into which a vast number of particular theories can be fitted. It claims *that* there are atoms, but leaves open an almost endless range of possibilities as to what they are like. This sort of contention may well be safe enough; at this level of a schematic looseness scientific claims can of course achieve security. But they do so only at the expense of definiteness—of that generality and precision which reflect what real science is all about.

5.2. The Basis of Metaphysical Realism

Behind the physical realism of science there stands a generic metaphysical realism that claims the objective reality of physical existents. But what is involved with this ontological mode of objecthood? To what are we committing ourselves in saying of something that it is 'a real thing', an object existing as an authentically real component of the physical world's furniture? Clearly, we stand committed to several (obviously interrelated) points:

1. *Substantiality of entity.* Being a something (entity) with its own unity of being. Having an established identity of its own.
2. *Physicality or reality.* Existing in space and time. Having a place as an actual concrete item in the world's physical scheme.
3. *Publicity or accessibility.* Admitting a shared commonality of access. Being something that different investigators proceeding from different points of departure can get hold of.
4. *Autonomy or independence.* Being independent of mind. Being something that observers find rather than create, that minds encounter rather than contrive.

The first two of these interrelated factors are purely ontological; but the second two have an epistemological aspect. And the two pairs are interconnected. In rational inquiry and natural science in particular, we try to get at the objective matters of fact regarding physical reality in ways that are accessible to all observers alike. (The repeatability of experiments is crucial.) And another salient factor enters in with that fourth and final issue—autonomy—in that the very idea of a real thing so functions in our conceptual scheme that actually existing things are thought of as having an identity, a nature, and a mode of comportment wholly indifferent to the cognitive state of the art regarding them—and potentially even very different from our own current conceptions of the matter. The issue of objectivity in the sense of mind-independence is pivotal for a viable realism. A fact is objective in this mode if it obtains thought-independently—if any change merely in what is thought by the world's intelligences would leave it unaffected. With objective facts (unlike matters of intersubjective agreement) what thinkers happen to think just does not enter in—what is at issue is thought-invariant or thought-indifferent. What realism maintains from the outset—and traditional idealism often struggles valiantly to retain (with mixed success)—is just this idea that there are certain objective facts that obtain thought-independently—irrespective of what we, or anybody else, think of them.

And at this point the very imperfection of our knowledge obtains a crucial bearing on the issue of realism. The conception of a *thing* that underlies our discourse about the furnishings of this world accordingly reflects a certain tentativity and fallibilism—the implicit recognition that our own personal or even communal conception of particular things may, in general, be inadequate if not outright wrong in so far as its detail is concerned. Behind our thought about things there is always a tinge of wary scepticism that recognizes the possibility of error. The objectivity of real existents projects them beyond the reach of our subjectively conditioned information.

There is wisdom in Hamlet's dictum: 'There are more things in heaven and earth, Horatio...' The limits of our knowledge may be the limits of *our* world, but they are not the limits of *the* world. We do and must recognize the limitations of our cognition. We cannot justifiably equate reality with what can, in principle, be known by us, nor equate reality with what can, in principle, be expressed by our language. And what is true here for our sort of mind is true for any other sort of finite mind as well. Any physically realizable sort of particular cognizant being can only come to know a part or aspect of the real.

We thus reach an important conjuncture of ideas. The ontological autonomy of things—their objectivity and independence of the machinations of mind—is a crucial aspect of realism. And the fact that it lies at the very core of our conception of a real thing that such items project beyond the cognitive reach of mind betokens a concept-scheme fundamentally committed to objectivity. Further or different facts concerning a real thing can always come to light, and all that we *do* say about it does not exhaust all that can and should be said about it. In this light, objectivity is crucial to realism and the cognitive inexhaustibility of things is a sure token of their objectivity.

However, an authentic realism can only exist in a state of tension. The only reality worth having is one that is in some degree knowable. But it is the very limitation of our knowledge—our recognition that there is more to reality than what we do and can ever know or even conjecture about it—that speaks for the mind-independence of the real. It is thus important to stress against the sceptic that the human mind is sufficiently well attuned to reality that *some* knowledge of it is possible. But it is no less important to join with realists in stressing the independent character of reality, acknowledging that reality has a depth and complexity of make-up that outruns the reach of any and all finite minds.

Peirce and others have located the impetus to realism in the limitations of man's will—in the fact that we can exert no control over our experience and, try as we will, cannot affect what we see and sense. Peirce's celebrated 'Harvard Experiment' of the Lowell Lectures of 1903 makes the point forcibly:

I know that this stone will fall if it is let go, because experience has convinced me that objects of this kind always do fall; and if anyone present has any doubt on the subject, I should be happy to try the experiment, and I will bet him a hundred to one on the result ... [I know this because of an unshakable conviction that] the uniformity with which stones have fallen has been due to some *active general principle* [of nature] ... Of course, every sane man will adopt the latter hypothesis. If he could doubt it in the case of the stone— which he can't—and I may as well drop the stone once and for all—I told you so!—if anybody doubt this still, a thousand other such inductive predictions are getting verified every day, and he will have to suppose every one of them to be merely fortuitous in order reasonably to escape the conclusion that *general principles are really operative in nature.* That is the doctrine of scholastic realism.[7]

[7] C. S. Peirce, *Collected Papers* (Cambridge, Mass.: Harvard University Press, 1931–58), v. s. 5.64–7. Compare also ii. s. 2.138, and: 'Whenever I've come to know a fact, it is by its resisting us. A man may walk down Wall Street debating within himself the existence of an external world; but in his brown study he jostles against somebody who angrily draws off and knocks him down. The sceptic is unlikely to carry his scepticism so far as to doubt whether anything besides the Ego was concerned in that phenomenon. The resistance shows that something independent of him is there. When anything strikes upon the senses the mind's train of thought is interrupted, for if it were not, nothing would distinguish the new observation from a fancy' (ibid. i. s. 1.431).

However, such a case for realism based on the deficiencies of causal control—the limits of the human will—fails to provide a telling argument for mind-independence seeing that dreams also lie outside people's control. A yet more potent impetus to realism lies in the limitations of man's *intellect,* pivoting on the circumstance that the features of real things inevitably outrun our cognitive reach. In placing further crucial aspects of the real altogether outside the effective range of present information, it speaks for a position that sees mind-independence as a salient feature of the real. The very fact of fallibilism and limitedness—of the realization that our putative knowledge does not do justice to the real truth of the matter of what reality is actually like—is surely one of the best arguments for a realism that pivots on the basic idea that there is more to reality than we humans do or can know about. It is the very limitation of our knowledge of things—our acknowledgment that reality extends beyond the horizons of what we can possibly know or even conjecture about—that most effectively betokens our recognition of the mind-independence of the real. A world that is acknowledged to be inexhaustible by our minds cannot easily be seen to be a product of their operations.

A powerful impetus to realism thus roots in the limitations of our knowledge, pivoting on the circumstance that the features of real things inevitably outrun our reach. In placing some crucial aspects of the real altogether outside our cognitive range it leaves little alternative to acknowledging mind-independence as a salient feature of the real. By acknowledging that our putative knowledge does not do justice to the real truth regarding what reality is actually like, we obtain what is surely one of the best arguments for realism through the idea that there is more to reality than we humans do or can know about it. For if our cognitive powers do not adequately grasp 'the way things really are' then this very circumstance clearly bolsters the case for realism. The cognitive intractability of things is something about which, in principle, we cannot delude ourselves, since such delusion would illustrate rather than abrogate the fact of a reality independent of ourselves.

The acknowledged inadequacy of our knowledge is thus one of the most powerful arguments there can be for a reality out there that lies beyond the inadequate efforts of mind. A healthy scepticism regarding our putative knowledge is something that comes far easier to realists than to radical idealists of a post-Berkeleyan stripe. For it is the very limitation of our knowledge of things—our recognition that reality extends beyond the horizons of what we ourselves can possibly know or even conjecture about it—that decisively betokens the mind-independence of the real.

5.3. Ramifications of Metaphysical Realism

As we have seen, physical realism has two indispensable and inseparable constituents—the one existential and ontological, and the other cognitive and epistemic. The former maintains that there indeed is a real world—a realm of mind-independent, objective material reality. The latter maintains that we can secure adequate descriptive information about this mind-independent realm to some very partial extent. This second contention obviously presupposes the first. But how can that first, ontological thesis be secured?

Such a metaphysical realism is clearly not an inductive inference secured through the scientific systematization of our observations, but rather represents a regulative presupposition that makes science possible in the first place. If we did not assume from the very outset that our sensations somehow relate to an extra-mental reality, we could clearly make no use of them to draw any inference whatever about 'the real world'. Experience would then lack any and all evidential bearing.

The realm of mind-independent reality is something we cannot *discover*—we do not learn that it exists as a result of inquiry and investigation. How could we ever learn from our observations that our mental experience is itself largely the causal product of the machinations of a mind-independent manifold, that all those phenomenal appearances are causally rooted in a physical reality? Will-independence comes easily enough, but thought-independence is harder to come by. This is clearly something we do not *learn* from inquiry because it is, all too clearly, a precondition for empirical inquiry—a presupposition for the usability of observational data as sources of objective information. That experience is indeed objective, that what we take to be evidence *is* evidence, that our sensations yield information about an order of existence outside the experiential realm itself, and that this experience constitutes not just a mere phenomenon but an appearance of something extra-mental belonging to an objectively self-subsisting order. All this is something that we must always presuppose in using experiential data as evidence for how things stand in the world. Such objectivity represents a postulation made on functional rather than evidential grounds: we endorse it in order to be in a position to learn by experience at all.

Accordingly, the crucial existential (ontological) component of realism is not a matter of discovery, a part of the findings of empirical research. It is a presupposition for our inquiries rather than a result thereof. We do not learn or discover that there is a mind-independent physical reality, we presume or postulate it. As Kant clearly saw, the objective world is presupposed from the outset rather than constituting an *ex post facto* discovery about the nature of things.[8] We have to do here with a formative assumption that undergirds our view of the nature of inquiry. Without subscribing to this idea, we just could not think of our knowledge as we actually do. Our commitment to the existence of a mind-independent reality is thus a postulate whose justification pivots—in the first instance at any rate—on its functional utility in enabling us to operate as we do with respect to inquiry.

Of course, after we postulate an objective reality in its concomitant causal aspect, then principles of inductive systematization, of explanatory economy, and of common cause consilience can work wonders towards furnishing us with plausible claims about various aspects of the nature of the real. Accordingly, that second, descriptive (epistemic) component of realism thus stands on a very different footing. Reality's *nature* is something about which we can only make warranted claims through examining it. Substantive information must come through inquiry—through evidential validation. Once we are willing to credit our observational data with objectivity, and thus with evidential bearing, then we can, of course, make use of them to inform ourselves as to the nature of the real. But we indispensably need that initial existential presupposition to make a start since without a commitment to a reality to serve as ground and object of our experience, its cognitive import would be lost. Only on its basis

---

[8] Kant held that we cannot experientially learn through perception about the objectivity of outer things, because we can only recognize our perceptions as *perceptions* (i.e. representations of outer things) if these outer things are supposed as such from the first (rather than being learned or inferred). As he summarizes in the 'Refutation of Idealism': 'Idealism assumed that the only immediate experience is inner experience, and that from it we can only *infer* outer things—and this, moreover, only in an untrustworthy manner.... But in the above proof it has been shown that outer experience is really immediate....' (*Critique of Pure Reason*, B 276).

can we proceed evidentially with the exploration of the interpersonally public and objective domain of a physical world-order that we share in common.

With respect to our cognitive endeavours, 'man proposes and nature disposes', and nature does this in both senses of the term: it disposes *over* our current view of reality and it will doubtless eventually dispose *of* it as well. Our view of the nature of inquiry and of the sort of process it represents is possible only because we stand committed from the very outset to the conception of ourselves as a minuscule component of a mind-independent reality. We can act and affect a few things in it, but in the main it has the whip hand and we merely respond to its causal dictates. And this is true in cognitive aspects as well—where we must simply do the best we can with the relatively feeble means at our disposal.

The only reasonable course is to heed Charles S. Peirce's pivotal injunction never to bar the path of inquiry. Our commitment to realism pivots on a certain practical *modus operandi*, encapsulated in the precept: 'Proceed in matters of inquiry and communication on the basis that you are dealing with an objective realm, existing quite independently of the doings and dealings of minds.' And on this basis we also standardly operate on the presumption of objectivity reflected in the guiding precept: 'Unless you have good reason to think otherwise (that is, as long as *nihil obstat*) treat the materials of inquiry and communication as veridical—as representing the nature of the real.' The ideal of objective reality is the focus of a family of serviceable regulative principles, affording a functionally useful instrument that enables us to transact our cognitive business in the most effective and satisfactory way.

Our realistic endorsement of unobserved causes in nature is thus not based on science but on metaphysics. What we learn from science is not *that* an unobservable order of physical existence causally undergirds nature as we observe it, but rather *what* these underlying structures are like. Science does not (cannot) teach us that the observable order is explicable in terms of underlying causes and that the phenomena of observation are signs or symptoms of this extra- and sub-phenomenal order of existence; we know this a priori of any world in which observation as we understand it can transpire. (After all, observations are, by their very nature, results of intentions.) What science does teach us (and metaphysics cannot) is what the descriptive character of this extra-phenomenal order is.

5.4. Realism in Pragmatic Perspective

But what considerations serve to legitimate metaphysical realism's postulation that experience affords data regarding an objective and mind-independent domain and thereby provides for viable information about the real? Given that the existence of such a domain is not a product of but a precondition for empirical inquiry, its acceptance has to be validated in the manner appropriate for postulates and prejudgements of any sort—namely in terms of its ultimate utility. Bearing this pragmatic perspective in mind, let us take a closer look at this issue of utility and ask what this postulation of a mind-independent reality can actually do for us.

The answer is straightforward. The assumption of a mind-independent reality is essential to the whole of our standard conceptual scheme relating to inquiry and communications. Without it, both the actual conduct and the rational legitimation of our communicative and investigative (evidential) practice would be destroyed. Nothing that we do in this cognitive domain would make sense if we did not subscribe to the conception of a mind-independent reality from the very outset.

To begin with, we indispensably require the notion of reality to operate the classical concept of truth as 'agreement with reality' (*adaequatio ad rem*). Once we abandon the concept of reality, the idea that in accepting a factual claim as true we become committed to how matters actually stand—'how it really is'—would also go by the board. The very semantics of our discourse constrain its commitment to realism; we have no alternative but to regard as real those states of affairs claimed by the contentions we are prepared to accept. Once we put a contention forward by way of serious assertion, we must view as real the states of affairs it purports, and must see its claims as facts. A factual statement on the order of 'There are pi mesons' is true if and only if the world is such that pi mesons exist within it. By virtue of their very nature as truths, true statements must state facts: they state what really is so, which is exactly what it is to characterize reality. The conceptions of *truth* and of *reality* come together in the notion of *adaequatio ad rem*—the venerable principle that to speak truly is to say how matters stand in reality, in that things actually are as we have said them to be.

In the second place, a nihilistic denial that there is such a thing as reality would destroy once and for all the crucial Parmenidean divide between appearance and reality. And this would exact a fearful price from us: we would be reduced to talking only of what we (I, you, many of us) *think* to be so. The crucial contrast notion of the *real* truth would no longer be available: we would only be able to contrast our *putative* truths with those of others, but could no longer operate the classical distinction between the putative and the actual, between what people merely think to be so and what actually is so. We could not take the stance that, as the Aristotelian commentator Themistius put it, 'that which exists does not conform to various opinions, but rather the correct opinions conform to that which exists'.[9]

The third point is the issue of cognitive co-ordination. Communication and inquiry, as we actually carry them on, are predicated on the fundamental idea of a real world of objective things that provide a common focus through existing and functioning in themselves, without specific dependence on ourselves and thereby equally accessible to others. Intersubjectively valid communication can be based only on common access to an objective order of things. The whole communicative project is predicated on a commitment to the idea that there is a realm of shared objects about which we as a community share questions and beliefs, and about which we ourselves as individuals presumably have only imperfect information that can be criticized and augmented by the efforts of others.

This points to a fourth important consideration. Only through reference to the real world as a *common object* and shared focus of our diverse and imperfect epistemic strivings are we able to effect communicative contact with one another. Inquiry and communication alike are geared to the conception of an objective world: a communally shared realm of things that exist strictly 'on their own' comprising an enduring and independent realm within which and, more importantly, with reference to which inquiry proceeds. We could not proceed on the basis of the notion that inquiry estimates the character of the real if we were not prepared to presume or postulate a reality for these estimates to be estimates of. It would clearly be pointless to devise our characterizations of reality if we did not stand committed to the proposition that there is a reality to be characterized.

The fifth item is a recourse to mind-independent reality that makes possible a realistic view of our knowledge as potentially

---

[9] Maimonides, *The Guide for the Perplexed*, 1. 71. 96a.

flawed. A rejection of this commitment to reality *an sich* (or to the actual truth about it) exacts an unacceptable price. For in abandoning this commitment we also lose those regulative contrasts that canalize and condition our view of the nature of inquiry (and indeed shape our conception of this process as it stands within the framework of our conceptual scheme). We could no longer assert: 'What we have there is good enough as far as it goes, but it is presumably not the whole real truth of the matter.' The very conception of inquiry as we conceive it would have to be abandoned if the contrast-facilitative conceptions of 'actual reality' and 'the real truth' were no longer available. Without the conception of reality we could not think of our knowledge in the fallibilistic mode we actually use—as having provisional, tentative, improvable features that constitute a crucial part of the conceptual scheme within whose orbit we operate our concept of inquiry.

Reality (on the traditional metaphysicians' construction of the concept) is the condition of things answering to 'the real truth'; it is the realm of what really is as it really is. The pivotal contrast is between mere appearance and reality as such, between our picture of reality and reality itself, between what actually is and what we merely think (believe, suppose, etc.) to be. And our allegiance to the conception of reality, and to this contrast that pivots upon it, root in the fallibilistic recognition that at the level of the detailed specifics of scientific theory, anything we presently hold to be the case may well turn out otherwise—indeed will surely do so if past experience gives any auguries for the future.

Our commitment to the mind-independent reality of 'the real world' stands together with our acknowledgment that, in principle, any or all of our *present* scientific ideas as to how things work in the world, at *any* present, may well prove to be untenable. Our conviction in a reality that lies beyond our imperfect understanding of it (in all the various senses of 'lying beyond') roots in our sense of the imperfections of our scientific world-picture—its tentativity and potential fallibility. In abandoning our commitment to a mind-independent reality, we would lose the impetus of inquiry.

Sixthly and finally, we require the conception of reality to operate the causal model of inquiry about the real world. Our standard picture of man's place in the scheme of things is predicated on the fundamental idea that there is a real world (however imperfectly our inquiry may characterize it) whose causal operations produce *inter alia* causal impacts upon us, providing the basis of our world-picture. Physical reality is viewed as the causal source and basis of the appearances, the originator and determiner of the phenomena of our cognitively relevant experience. 'The real world' is seen as causally operative both in serving as the external moulder of thought and as constituting the ultimate arbiter of the adequacy of our theorizing.

Our commitment to an objective reality lying behind the data at hand is indispensably demanded by any step into the domain of the publicly accessible objects essential to communal inquiry and interpersonal communication about a shared world. We could not establish communicative contact about a common objective item of discussion if our discourse were geared to the substance of our own idiosyncratic ideas and conceptions. But the objectivity at issue in our communicative discourse is a matter of its status rather than one of its content. For the substantive content of a claim about the world in no way tells us whether this claim is factual or fictional. That is something that we have to determine from its context: it is a matter of the frame, not of the canvas.

The conception of a mind-independent reality accordingly plays a central and indispensable role in our thinking with respect to matters of language and cognition. In communication and inquiry alike we seek to offer answers to our questions about how matters stand in this 'objective realm'. It is seen as the epistemological *object* of veridical cognition, in the context of the contrast between 'the real' and its 'merely phenomenal' appearances. Again, it is seen as the target or *telos* of the truth-estimation process at issue in inquiry, providing for a common focus in communication and communal inquiry. (The 'real world' thus constitutes the 'object' of our cognitive endeavours in both senses of this term—the objective at which they are directed and the purpose for which they are exerted.) And further, reality is seen as the ontological *source* of cognitive endeavours, affording the existential matrix in which we move and have our being, and whose impact upon us is the prime mover for our cognitive efforts. All of these facets of the concept of reality are integrated and unified in the classical doctrine of truth as it corresponds to fact (*adaequatio ad rem*), a doctrine that makes sense only in the setting of a commitment to mind-independent reality.

In the end, then, the justification for the fundamental presupposition of objectivity is not evidential at all; postulates are not based on evidence. Rather, it is functional. We need this postulate to operate our conceptual scheme. The justification of this postulate lies in its utility. We could not form our existing conceptions of truth, fact, inquiry, and communication without presupposing the independent reality of an external world. We simply could not think of experience and inquiry as we do. (What we have here is a transcendental argument of sorts from the character of our conceptual scheme to the acceptability of its inherent presuppositions.) The primary validation of that crucial objectivity postulate roots in its basic functional utility in relation to our cognitive aims. For—to summarize—we need that postulate of an objective order of mind-independent reality for at least six important reasons.

1. To preserve the distinction between true and false with respect to factual matters and to operate the idea of truth as agreement with reality.

2. To preserve the distinction between appearance and reality, between our picture of reality and reality itself.

3. To serve as a basis for intersubjective communication.

4. To furnish the basis for a shared project of communal inquiry.

5. To provide for the fallibilistic view of human knowledge.

6. To sustain the causal mode of learning and inquiry and to serve as basis for the objectivity of experience.

Only in subscribing to that fundamental reality postulate can we maintain the view of experience, inquiry, and communication with which we in fact operate. Without it, the entire conceptual framework of our thinking about the world and our place within it would come crashing down. It is a conception of indispensable utility.

Yet crucial though this may be, it clearly cannot be the entire story. The consideration that we *must* proceed in the way of objectivity-presuming cognition as a matter of the functional requisites of our situation does not offer us any assurance that we will actually succeed, it just has it that we will not if we do not. And so, a nagging doubt still remains. It roots in the following challenge:

Let us grant that this line of approach provides a cogent practical argument. All this shows is that realism is indispensably *useful*. But does that make it *true*? Is there any rational warrant for it over and above the mere fact of its utility?

At this point we have to move beyond presupposed functional requisites to address the issue of actual effectiveness. We must now have recourse to the resources of actual experience. For what *is* learned by experience—and can only be learned in this way—is that in proceeding on this prejudgement our attempts do, by and large, work out pretty well *vis-à-vis* the purposes we have in view for inquiry and communication. When we treat certain data as evidence we extend evidential credit to them, as it were. Through trial and error we learn that some of them do indeed *deserve* it, and then we proceed to extend to them greater weight—we increase their credit limit and rely on them more extensively. And to use those data properly as evidence is to build up a picture of the world, a picture which shows, with the wisdom of hindsight, how appropriate it was for us to use those evidential data in the first place.

Accordingly, the substantive picture of nature's ways that is secured through our empirical inquiries is itself ultimately justified, retrospectively as it were, through affording us with the presuppositions on whose basis inquiry proceeds. As we develop science there must come a closing of the circle: its findings must ultimately serve to legitimate its methods. The world-picture that a cogently developed science delivers into our hands must eventually become such as to explain how it is that creatures such as ourselves, emplaced in the world as we are, investigating it by the processes we actually use, should do fairly well at developing a workable view of that world.[10] The validation of scientific method must in the end itself rest on a scientific basis. For our knowledge claims to be viable, science must (and can) retrovalidate itself—with the wisdom of hindsight—by providing the material (in terms of a science-based world-view) for rationalizing the methods of science themselves. The complex cyclic picture of the previous chapter comes into play here. And though the process is cyclic and circular, there is nothing vicious and vitiating about it. Instead, the closing of these inquiry-geared loops validates, retrospectively, those realistic presuppositions or postulations that made the whole process of inquiry possible in the first place. Realism thus emerges as a presupposition-affording postulate for inquiry— albeit one whose ultimate legitimation emerges retrospectively through the results, both practical and cognitive, that the process of inquiry based on those yet-to-be-justified presuppositions is able to achieve.

[10] Not that this shows that science gets it right, but only (1) that science does not get it so badly wrong that efficacy is compromised, and (2) that science progresses—that the science of a late day stands on a securer footing than that of earlier times.

6

Intimations of Idealism

SYNOPSIS

*(1) The fact that the world's real things are cognitively inexhaustible—
that we can never manage to say all that can and should be said about
them—means that it is neither necessary nor desirable to speak of an
opposition between realism and idealism. (2) For plausible versions of
these two positions can actually be combined, and, in particular, metaphysical realism is fully compatible with conceptual idealism. (3) On the
other hand, a hardline ontological idealism is unacceptable: man is not
necessarily the measure of the real.*

6.1. Combining Metaphysical Realism with Conceptual Idealism

We cannot lay credible claim to cognitive monopoly or cognitive
finality regarding the things of this world. For an unavoidable recognition of the incompleteness and imperfection of our information
regarding the detail of things is inherent in the very nature of our
conception of a 'real thing'. Our epistemic stance towards the real
world commits us to recognize that every part and parcel of it has
features lying beyond our present cognitive reach—at *any* 'present'
whatsoever. And much the same story holds when our concern is not
with physical things, but with *types* of such things. To say that
something is copper or magnetic is to say more than that it has the
properties we think copper or magnetic things have; it is to say that
this thing *is* copper or magnetic with all of the as-yet-undiscovered
ramifications of fact. And this means also that we must be prepared
to contemplate the prospect that we have it wrong in matters of
detail.

The point is that our only cognitive access to real objects is via our
conceptions of them, and that these conceptions (1) are always

incomplete in various ways, and (2) will often if not generally be in some ways incorrect—though in neither case can we as yet identify the imperfection at issue. Yet we stand committed to the idea that the imperfection of our conception of the objects is not thereby prevented from being one *of that object*—that is, that those inadequacies do not matter for the appropriateness of the identification of the object. However, this is something we do not know but can only presume—a presumption that is based on practical rather than evidential grounds.

The ontological thesis that there is a mind-independent physical reality to which our inquiries address themselves with but imperfect adequacy is a key element of metaphysical realism. The preceding deliberations have argued that this basic thesis has the epistemic status of a presuppositional postulate that is initially validated by its pragmatic utility and ultimately retrovalidated through the results of its implementation in both theoretical inquiry and practical application. Our commitment to metaphysical realism is, on this account, initially based not on the product of our *inquiries* about the world, but upon a crucial facet of how we *conceive* the world that we inquire about. Clearly, then, such a realism itself rests on an idealistic basis. Ultimately, it does not represent a discovered fact, but a methodological presupposition of our praxis of inquiry; it is not constitutive (fact-descriptive) but regulative (praxis-facilitating). It is a position to which we are constrained not by the push of evidence but by the pull of purpose—not a factual discovery but a practical postulate justified by its utility or serviceability in the context of our aims and purposes. For if we did not *take* our experience to serve as an indication of facts about an objective order we would not be able to validate any objective claims whatsoever. Such a position—realistic though it is—is deeply idealistic in nature, established by considering, as a matter of practical reasoning, how we do (and must) think about the world within the context of the projects to which we stand committed.

However, this sort of idealism is not substantive but methodological. It is not a denial of real objects that exist independently of mind and as such are causally responsible for our objective experience. Quite the reverse, it is designed to facilitate their acceptance. But it insists that the justifactory *rationale* for this acceptance roots in considerations of mind-supplied purpose rather than empirical/factual discovery. For on its telling our commitment to mind-independent reality arises not *from* experience but *for* it—i.e. for the sake of our being in a position to exploit our experience to ground inquiry and communication with respect to the objectively real. A position of this sort is in business as a realism all right. But seeing that it pivots on the character of our concepts and their *modus operandi*, it transpires that the business premises it occupies are to some extent mortgaged to idealism. The fact that a meaningful realism has to be a realism of things as we conceive them to be allows idealism to infiltrate into the realist's domain. Such a position sees this commitment to a mind-independent reality in an essentially utilitarian role—as a functional requisite for our intellectual resources (specifically for our conceptual scheme in relation to communication and inquiry). Thanks to its enmeshment in considerations of aims and purposes, it is clear that this sort of commitment to an objectivistic realism harks back to the salient contention of classical idealism that values and purposes play a pivotal role in our understanding of the nature of things. We arrive, paradoxical as it may seem, at a realism that is founded—initially at least—on a *justificatory basis* whose purport and tendency is substantially idealistic in a way that makes it neither necessary nor desirable to speak of an unqualified conflict or opposition here.

6.2. The Dialectic of Realism and Idealism

An all-out realism, as we have seen, embraces the following theses:

1. There is a mind-independent physical reality which, as such, has a descriptive nature of some sort.

2. We can know something about it—we can acquire (a substantial volume of) accurate information about the nature of the real.

3. The descriptive knowledge of reality afforded us by natural science characterizes it as it is in itself—in terms of references that do not hinge on some particular cognitive perspective, being independent of the particular ways and means used by inquirers in forming their picture of the real.

Owing to the internal complexity of such a doctrine, there will be various stages to the realism/idealism controversy and very different versions of the realism or idealism.

(a) The issue of *metaphysical* realism/idealism hinges on the acceptance of (1) itself.

(b) The issue of *cognitive* realism/idealism hinges on whether one is prepared to go beyond (1) so far as to accept (2) as well.

(c) The issue of *scientific* realism/idealism hinges on whether one is prepared to go beyond (2) to accept (3) as well.

The overall position that has been defended here is that realism is plausible through point (2) and ceases to be so at (3).

What is right about idealism is inherent in the fact that in investigating the real we are clearly constrained to use our own concepts to address our own issues—that we can only learn about the real in our own terms of reference. All that reality will ever provide us with are answers to the questions we put to it. But what is right about realism is that the answers to the questions we put to the real are provided by reality itself—whatever the answers may be, they are what they are because it is reality itself that determines them to be that way. Intelligence proposes but reality disposes.

The realist holds the existence and nature of reality to be mind-independent. But independent of *whose* mind? One can, in theory, maintain such a position in different ways, holding that real things are mind-independent only in the sense of existing independently of:

• my conceptions of them
• our current (communal, societally current) conceptions
• anybody's conception ever, among our fellow humans
• their conceivability-in-principle by finite intelligences
• God's conception of them.

As we move down this list, the position we take becomes increasingly more problematic. At the outset we start with the rejection of megalomania. Well and good! But by the end we reject Peirce's condemnation of incognizables, and this is something far more questionable. To accept the existence of things that cannot *in principle* be known—things which by their very nature lie outside the range of any and every (hypothetically possible) intelligence—is strong stuff.

Compare and contrast the following three theses:

• To be real is to be recognized as such by a (real) mind—i.e. to exist *for* an actual mind.
• To be real is to be recognizable as such by a (finite possible) mind—to be accessible to a (possible finite) mind.
• To be known to be real is to be known to be such by a mind.

The first of these theses represents an *ontological* idealism ('to exist is to exist for a mind'). And the third thesis is a mere trivial truism (only mind-endowed beings can, by hypothesis, know anything). But the second represents a distinct intermediate position—a *cognitive* idealism that holds that the appropriate explanation of what it is for something to exist physically must be given in terms that make reference to mind.[1] And it is such a version of idealism that stands at the forefront of our present discussion. This is a realism all right, since it acknowledges a realm of ontological mind-independent existence. But since it stands committed to a cognizability-in-principle standard of real/true/actual it is also an idealism that holds that the commitment to real existence is to be explicated and validated in mind-referring terms of reference.

The salient point to emerge from such deliberations is that the realism/idealism debate is rendered complex through the great variety of realisms and opposing idealisms that can be contemplated. When one considers the controversy in detached perspective, one is led to the recognition that there is no prospect of a one-sided victory here. The sensible move is to opt for the middle ground and to combine a plausible version of realism with a plausible version of idealism. The issue is not one of the dichotomous choice of *either* realism *or* idealism, but rather one of a compromise in the interests of fruitful collaboration between these historically warring positions.

It is quite unjust to charge such an idealism with an antipathy to reality, with *ontophobia*, as Ortega y Gasset called it. For it is not the existence but the nature of reality upon which idealism sets its sights, holding that something exists if there is potential experiential access to it—if something indeed exists in the world, then it must be observable-in-principle, detectable by a suitably endowed creature equipped with some suitably powerful technology.

6.3. Who is the Arbiter of Reality? Is Man the Measure?

Whatever can be known by us humans to be real must of course actually be real in virtue of this very fact. But does the converse hold? Is humanly cognizable reality the only sort of reality there it? Some

---

[1] For a fuller development of the implications of such a position, see the author's *Conceptual Idealism* (Oxford: Blackwell, 1973).

philosophers certainly say so, even maintaining that there actually is a fact of the matter only when a claim to this effect is such that 'we [humans] could in finite time bring ourselves into a position in which we were justified either in asserting or in denying [it]'.[2] On such a view reality is *our* human reality. What we humans are not in a position to domesticate cognitively—what we cannot bring to realization by (finite!) cognitive effort—simply does not exist as a part of reality at all. Where we have no cognitive access, there just is nothing to be accessed. We are led back to the *homo mensura* doctrine of Protagoras: 'Man is the measure of all things, of what is, that it is, or what is not, that it is not.'

But there are big problems here. Berkeley maintained that 'to be (real) is to be perceived' (*esse est percipi*). This does not seem all that plausible. It seems more sensible to adopt 'to be is to be perceivable' (*esse est percipile esse*). For Berkeley, of course, this was a distinction without a difference: if it is perceivable at all, then God perceives it. But if we embargo philosophical reliance on God, the matter looks different. We are then driven back to the question of what is perceivable for perceivers who are physically realizable in the real world. And so, something really exists if it is, in principle, experientiable: 'To be (physically) real is to be the possible object of perception of a possible perceiver—one who is physically realizable in the world.' *Physical* existence is seen as tantamount to observability-in-principle. The basic idea is that one can only claim (legitimately or appropriately) that a particular physical object exists if there is experiential access to it—not necessarily for us but for some experience-capable sort of creature.

On this approach, one would endorse the idea that to be part of physical reality is to be:

• not necessarily observed, but observable;
• not necessarily perceived, but perceivable;
• not necessarily experienced, but experientiable.[3]

And all these 'ables' have to be generally construed as regards the beings who bear the abilities and capacities at issue. To exist (physically) is to be part of the world's causal commerce—to be at the

---

[2] Michael Dummett, 'Truth', *Proceedings of the Aristotelian Society*, 59 (1958–9), 160.

[3] Note that we cannot say, 'To be is to be describable', or 'To be is to be identifiable,' since purely hypothetical possibilities can also be described and identified. What they cannot be is *experienced* by some physically realizable intelligence.

initiating or receiving end of a causal process that can, in principle, be detected and monitored by an attentive intelligence. On such an approach, to exist (physically) is thus to be 'observable' in principle—to be open to experiential confrontation by a cognition-capable creature of some sort. And such merely dispositional observability is clearly something *objective*, in contrast to actual observations, which are always personalized. Observability is a matter of what beings with mind-endowed capacities *can* encounter in experience, and not one of what any particular one or more of them actually *does* encounter in experience. And it is clear that such a weak—and cognitive rather than ontological—version of substantival idealism is altogether unproblematic.

It is true that the shift from Berkeley's 'To be is to be perceived' to our presently contemplated 'To be is to be experientiable' still leaves us with some problems. Prime among them is the question, just who is to be at issue here? We can attenuate, of course, the fact/cognition distinction by liberalizing the cognizers at issue. Consider the following series of contentions: *For something to be a fact it is necessary that it be knowable by:*

1. Oneself
2. One's contemporary (human) fellow inquirers
3. Us humans (at large and in the long run)
4. Some actual species of intelligent creatures
5. *Some physically realizable (though not necessarily actual) type of intelligent being—creatures conceivably endowed with cognitive resources far beyond our feeble human powers*
6. An omniscient being (i.e. God)

On this approach, the idealist emerges as the exponent of a verifiability theory of reality, equating truth and reality with what is verifiable by 'us'—with different, and increasingly liberal constructions of just who is to figure in that 'us group'. The i-th level idealist maintains, and the i-th-level realist denies such a thesis at the i-th entry on the list. But just how is one to appraise these positions?

Where one sets the boundary in interpreting the idealist doctrine that to be real is to be cognizable will determine the sort of idealism that is at issue. No sensible idealist maintains a position as strong as (1). No sensible realist denies a position as weak as (6). The salient question is just where to draw the line in determining what is a viable realistic/idealistic position.

Let us focus upon case (3), the man-is-the-measure, *homo mensura*, doctrine. Of course, what we humans can *know* to be real will (*ex hypothesi*) constitute a part or aspect of reality-at-large. That much is not in question. The bone of contention between *homo mensura* realism and idealism is the question of a surplus—of whether reality may have sectors or aspects that outrun the reach of human cognition. By *this* standard, both Peirce and the Dummett of the earlier quotation are clearly *homo mensura* realists, seeing that both (quite implausibly) confine the real to what *people*—members of *Homo sapiens*—can come to know. But this is not all that realistic (in the other sense of the term). Man may be the measurer of the real, but he is not its measure: his proceedings do not determine what the outcome of the measured process is, that elephants outweigh mice has nothing to do with us.

It seems sensible to take the stance that a naturally evolved mind will—thanks to evolution itself—have a sufficiently close alignment to reality as to be able to secure some knowledge of it. But on the other hand it does not seem plausible that reality has no reserve surplus of fact and has no aspects that are not domesticated within the cognitive range of existing creatures (let alone one particular species thereof!). It thus seems sensible to adopt the idealistic line only at level (5), and to be a realist short of that. One would, accordingly, take the view that to be real is to be causally active—to be a part of the world's causal commerce. And since one can always hypothesize a creature that detects a given sort of causal process, we need not hesitate to equate reality with experientiability in principle. We thus arrive at the level (5) idealism, one of the very weakest viable sorts. At all the lower-numbered, more substantive levels our present position is effectively realistic.

A qualified realism of this somewhat halfway-house sort holds that what is so as a matter of fact is not necessarily cognizable by 'us' no matter how far within the limits of plausibility we extend the boundaries of that us-community of inquiring intelligences, as long as we remain within the limits of the actual. Any particular sort of possible cognizing being can know only a part or aspect of reality. But the situation changes when we move from *any* to *all*. One cannot make plausible sense of 'such-and such a feature of nature is real but no possible sort of intelligent being could possibly discern it'. To be real is to be in a position to make an impact somewhere on something of such a sort that a suitably equipped, mind-endowed, intelligent creature could detect it. What is real in the world must make some difference to it that is, in principle, detectable. Existence-in-this-world is co-ordinated with perceivability-in-principle. And so, at this point, there is a concession to idealism.

In any case, *homo mensura* realism is untenable. It would be altogether implausible to see man as the measure here. There is no good reason to manifest a hubris that sees our human reality as the only one there is. After all, humans have the capacity not only for knowledge but also for imagination. And it is simply too easy for us to conceive of a realm of things and states of things of which we can obtain no knowledge because 'we have no way to get there from here', lacking the essential means for securing information in such a case. Neither astronomically nor otherwise are we the centre around which all things revolve. A *homo mensura* realism which limits the 'that' and the 'what' of real existence to the realm of human knowledge is ultimately implausible.

But let us now look more closely at the complex issue of nature's intelligibility through the instrumentalities of science.[4]

---

[4] Further issues relevant to this chapter's deliberations are discussed in the author's *Scientific Realism* (Dordrecht: D. Reidel, 1987).

7

The Intelligibility of Nature

SYNOPSIS

(1) The intelligibility of nature—the rational comprehensibility of the real, so to speak—is often characterized as a great mystery. (2) Such a position is very questionable because nature and its investigators actually collaborate in bringing this condition of affairs to realization. (3) We humans do our part in that our intelligence—like that of any other possible intelligent being—is the product of evolutionary development. (4–5) Nature does its part by making this development possible. (6) The inevitable conformity of these two factors dissolves the 'mystery'. (7) Evolution—broadly understood to include both natural and rational selection—provides the key here. To be sure, the mind–nature co-ordination at issue is limited in its scope, but there is good reason to think that it is more than adequate to accomplish the explanatory task that arises here.

7.1. The Cognitive Accessibility of Nature

How is it that natural science—and, in particular, physics—is possible at all? How is it that we humans, mere dust-specks on the world's immense stage, can manage to unlock nature's secrets and gain access to her laws? And how is it that our mathematics—seemingly a free creative invention of the human imagination—can be used to characterize the *modus operandi* of nature with such uncanny efficacy and accuracy? Why is it that the majestic lawful order of nature is intelligible to us humans in our man-devised conceptual terms?[1]

---

[1] This very Kantian issue will be treated here in a very un-Kantian way. For the present deliberations will not be addressed, *à la* Kant, to certain a priori principles that supposedly *underlie* physics. Rather, our tale will unfold in terms of the factual (a posteriori) principles that *constitute* physics—the laws of nature themselves.

As long as people thought of the world as the product of the creative activity of a mathematicizing intelligence, as the work of a creative demiurge or deity who proceeds *more mathematico* in the design of nature, the issue is wholly unproblematic. God endows nature with a mathematical order and mind with a duly consonant mathematicizing intelligence. There is thus no problem about how the two get together—the Creator simply fixes it that way. But, of course, if *this* is to be the canonical rationale for the human mind's grasp on nature's laws, then in forgoing explanatory recourse to God we also—to all appearances—lose our hold on the intelligibility of nature in humanly accessible terms.[2]

Accordingly some of the deepest intellects of recent times think that our hold on nature's intelligibility is gone forever. Various scientists and philosophers of the very first rank nowadays confidently affirm that we cannot hope to solve this puzzle of the intelligibility of nature in a mathematically lawful manner. Erwin Schroedinger characterizes the circumstance that man can discover the laws of nature as 'a miracle that may well be beyond human understanding'.[3] Eugene Wigner asserts that 'the enormous usefulness of mathematics in the natural sciences is something bordering on the mysterious, and there is no rational explanation for it'.[4] He goes on to wax surprisingly lyrical in maintaining that, 'The miracle of the appropriateness of the language of mathematics for the formulation of the laws of physics is a wonderful gift which we neither understand not deserve.'[5] Even Albert Einstein stood in awe before this problem. In a letter written in 1952 to an old friend of his Berne days, Maurice Solovine, he wrote:

You find it curious that I regard the intelligibility of the world (in the measure that we are authorized to speak of such an intelligibility) as a miracle or an eternal mystery. Well, *a priori* one should expect that the word be rendered lawful only to the extent that we intervene with our ordering intelligence ... [But] the kind of order, on the contrary, created, for example by Newton's theory of gravitation, is of an altogether different character. Even if the axioms of the theory are set by men, the success of such

---

[2] The medieval dictum *non in philosophia recurrere est ad deum* may be translated roughly as 'Do not call on God to pull your philosophical chestnuts out of the fire.'

[3] Erwin Schroedinger, *What is Life?* (Cambridge: Cambridge University Press, 1945), 31.

[4] Eugene P. Wigner, 'The Unreasonable Effectiveness of Mathematics in the Natural Sciences', *Communications on Pure and Applied Mathematics*, 13 (1960), 2.

[5] Ibid. 14.

an endeavor presupposed in the objective world a high degree of order that we were *a priori* in no way authorized to expect. This is the 'miracle' that is strengthened more and more with the development of our knowledge.... The curious thing is that we have to content ourselves with recognizing the 'miracle' without having a legitimate way of going beyond it...[6]

According to all these eminent physicists we are confronted here by a genuine mystery: the problem of nature's intelligibility through man's mathematical theorizing is seen as intractable. We have to acknowledge *that* nature is intelligible via our scientific inquiries, but we have no prospect of understanding *why* this is so. All three of these distinguished Nobel laureates in physics unblushingly employ the word 'miracle' in this connection.

Perhaps, then, the question is even illegitimate and should not be raised at all. Perhaps the issue of nature's intelligibility is not just intractable, but actually inappropriate and somehow based on a false presupposition. For to ask for an explanation as to why scientific inquiry is successful presupposes that there is a rationale for this fact. And if this circumstance is something fortuitous and accidental, then no such rationale exists at all. Just this position is preferred by various philosophers. For example, it is the line taken by Karl Popper, who writes:

[Traditional treatments of induction] all assume not only that our quest for [scientific] knowledge has been successful, but also that we should be able to explain why it is successful. However, even on the assumption (which I share) that our quest for knowledge has been very successful so far, and that we now know something of our universe, this success becomes [i.e. remains] miraculously improbable, and therefore inexplicable; for an approach at an endless series of improbable accidents is not an explanation. (The best we can do, I suppose, is to investigate the almost incredible evolutionary history of these accidents...)[7]

Mary Hesse, the English philosopher of science, also thinks that it is inappropriate to ask for an explanation of the success of science 'because science might, after all, be a miracle'.[8] On this sort of view, the question of the intelligibility of nature becomes an illegitimate pseudo-problem—a forbidden fruit at which sensible minds should

---

[6] Albert Einstein, *Lettres à Maurice Solovine* (New York: Philosophical Library, 1987), 114–15.

[7] K. R. Popper, *Objective Knowledge* (Oxford: Clarendon Press, 1972), 28.

[8] Mary Hesse, *Revolutions and Reconstructions in the Philosophy of Science* (Bloomington, Ind.: University of Indiana Press, 1980), 154.

not presume to nibble. We must simply remain content with the fact itself, realizing that any attempt to explain it is foredoomed to failure because of the inappropriateness of the very project.

And so, on this grand question of how the success of natural science is possible at all, some of the shrewdest intellects of the day avow themselves baffled, and unhesitatingly proceed to shroud the issue in mystery and incomprehension. Clearly, however, such a view is of questionable merit. Eminent authorities to the contrary notwithstanding, the question of nature's intelligibility through natural science is not only interesting and important, but also one which we should, in principle, hope to answer in a more or less sensible way. Surely, this issue needs and deserves a strong dose of demystification.

7.2. A Closer Look at the Problem

Let us begin at the beginning. How is it that we can make effective use of mathematical machinery to characterize the *modus operandi* of nature? How is mathematical exactness possible save under the supposition that 'science gets it right'?

The pure logician seems to have a ready answer. He says: 'Mathematics *must* apply to reality. Mathematical propositions are purely abstract truths whose validation turns on conceptual issues alone. Accordingly, they hold of this world because they hold of every possible world.' However, this response misses the point of present concerns. Admittedly, the truths of *pure* mathematics obtain in and of every possible world. But they do so only in virtue of the fact that they are strictly hypothetical and descriptively empty—wholly uncommitted regarding the substantive issues of the world's operations. Their very conceptual status means that the theses of pure mathematics are beside the point of our present purposes. It is not the a priori truth of pure mathematics that concerns us, its ability to afford truths of reason. Rather, what is at issue is the empirical applicability of mathematics, its pivotal and astonishingly effective role in framing the a posteriori, contingent truths of lawful fact that render nature's ways amenable to reason.

After all, the fact that pure mathematics obtains in a world does not mean that this world's *laws* have to be characterizable in relatively straightforward mathematical terms. It does not mean that nature's operations have to be congenial to mathematics and graspable in terms of simple, neat, elegant, and rationally accessible formulas. In short, it does not mean that the world must be mathematically tractable and 'mathematophile' in being receptive to the sort of descriptive treatment it receives in mathematical physics.

How, then, are we to account for the fact that the world appears to us to be so eminently intelligible in the mathematical terms of our theoretical science of nature?

The answer to this question of the cognitive accessibility of nature to mathematicizing intelligence has to lie in a somewhat complex, two-sided story in which both sides, intelligence and nature, must be expected to have a part. Let us trace out this line of thought—one step at a time.

For factual knowledge to arise at all, the beliefs of inquiring minds and the world's actual arrangements must be duly co-ordinated in mutual attunement. But when two parties agree, this can come about in very different ways. Consider two piles of rocks that correspond in size. Clearly, this might transpire because:

1. (1) is adjusted to (2). The size of (2) is the independent variable and that of (1) the dependent variable.

2. (2) is adjusted to (1) with the status of the two variables now reversed.

3. There is a two-way co-ordination, a reciprocal adjustment, a give-and-take coupling, an *interaction*.

Exactly the same spectrum of possibilities exists with respect to the issue of mind/reality co-ordination. Here too, there are three alternatives:

1. *Physicalism or ontological materialism*: In human knowledge, mind and extra-mental reality agree because extra-mental reality constrains the operations of mind along a one-way street with mental processes as the causally constrained products of an extra-mental reality.

2. *Ontological idealism*: In human knowledge, mind and extra-mental reality agree because mind actually *constructs* that seemingly extra-mental nature. Mind is in control, so that, in consequence, all else agrees with mind.

3. *Interactionism*: In human knowledge there is agreement between mental operations and extra-mental reality through a mutual accommodation engendering a process of give-and-take interaction, in the course of which our conceptions are co-ordinated with the

ways of extra-mental reality through the operation of evolutionary processes.

The third alternative clearly provides the most attractive option here—and the most viable one. To see why this is so let us examine more closely how the mind–nature co-ordination essential to a knowledge of natural fact actually arises.

7.3. 'Our' Side

One instructive way of approaching the problem from our side of the interaction is via the question, 'To what extent would the *functional equivalent* of natural science built up by the enquiring intelligences of an astronomically remote civilization of alien creatures be bound to resemble our science?' In reflecting on this question and its ramifications, one soon comes to realize that there is an enormous potential for diversity.

To begin with, the machinery of formulation used in expressing their science might be altogether different. Specifically, their mathematics might be very unlike ours. Their dealings with quantity might be entirely anumerical—purely comparative with regard to patterns, for example, rather than quantitative. Especially if their environment is not amply endowed with solid objects or stable structures congenial to measurement—if, for example, they were jellyfish-like creatures swimming about in a soupy sea—their geometry could be something rather strange, largely topological, say, and geared to flexible configurations rather than fixed sizes or shapes. Digital thinking might be undeveloped among digit-lacking creatures, while certain sorts of analogue reasoning might be highly refined. Or, again, an alien civilization might, like the ancient Greeks, have Euclidean geometry without analysis. But in any case, given that the mathematical mechanisms at their disposal could be very different from ours, it is clear that their description of nature in mathematical terms could also be very different. (Not necessarily truer or false, but just different.)

Secondly, the *orientation* of the science of an alien civilization might be very different. The interests of creatures shaped under the remorseless pressure of evolutionary adaptations to quite different— and endlessly variable—environmental conditions might well point their thought in directions totally unlike anything that is familiar to us. The science of a different civilization would inevitably be closely tied to the particular pattern of their interaction with nature as funnelled through the particular course of their evolutionary adjustment to their specific environment. The 'forms of sensibility' of radically different beings (to invoke Kant's useful idea) are likely to be radically diverse from ours. The direct chemical analysis of environmental materials might prove highly useful, and bioanalytic techniques akin to our senses of taste and smell could be very highly developed, providing them with environmentally oriented experiences of a very different sort. All their efforts might conceivably be devoted to the social sciences—to developing highly sophisticated analogues of psychology and sociology, for example. In particular, if the intelligent aliens were a diffuse assemblage of units comprising wholes in ways that allow of overlap,[9] then social concepts might become so paramount for them that nature would throughout be viewed in fundamentally social categories, with those aggregates we think of as physical structures contemplated by them in social terms.

Then, too, their natural science might deploy processual mechanisms quite different from ours. Communicating by means of some sort of telepathy based upon variable odours or otherwise exotic signals, they might devise a complex theory of emphatic thought-wave transmittal through an ideaferous aether. Again, the aliens might scan nature very differently. Electromagnetic phenomena might lie altogether outside the ken of alien life-forms; if their environment does not afford them lodestones and electrical storms, the occasion to develop electromagnetic theory might never arise. The course of scientific development tends to flow in the channel of practical interests. A society of porpoises might lack crystallography but develop a very sophisticated hydrodynamics; one comprised of mole-like creatures might never dream of developing optics or astronomy but have a very sophisticated sort of earth science. One's language and thought processes are bound to be closely geared to the world as one experiences it. As is illustrated by the difficulties we ourselves experience in bringing the language of everyday experience to bear on subatomic phenomena, our concepts are ill-attuned to facets of nature different in scale or structure from our own. We can

---

[9] Compare the discussion in Gösta Ehrensvärd, *Man on Another World* (Chicago: University of Chicago Press, 1965), 146–8.

hardly expect a science that reflects such parochial preoccupations to be a universal fixture.

Moreover, the conceptualization of an alien science might be nothing at all like our own. We must reckon with the theoretical possibility that a remote civilization might operate with a drastically different system of concepts in its cognitive dealings with nature. Different cultures and different intellectual traditions, to say nothing of different sorts of creatures, are bound to describe and explain their experience—their world as they conceive it—in terms of concepts and categories of understanding substantially different from ours. They would diverge radically in what Germans would call their *Denkmittel*—the conceptual instruments they employ in thought about the facts (or purported facts) of the world. They could, accordingly, be said to operate with different conceptual schemes, with different conceptual tools used to make sense of experience—to characterize, describe, and explain the items that figure in the world as they view it. The taxonomic and explanatory mechanisms by means of which their cognitive business is transacted might differ so radically from ours that intellectual contact with them would be difficult or impossible.

Laws are detectable regularities in nature. But detectable by whom? Detection will of course vary drastically with the mode of observation—that is, with the sort of resources that different creatures have at their disposal to do their detecting. Everything depends on how nature pushes back on our senses and their instrumental extensions. Even if we detect everything we can, we will not have got hold of everything available to others. And the converse is equally true. The laws that we (or anybody else) manage to formulate will depend crucially on one's place within nature—on how one is connected into its wiring diagram, so to speak.

A comparison of the 'science' of different civilizations here on earth suggests that it is not an outlandish hypothesis to suppose that the very topics of alien science might differ dramatically from those of ours. In our own case, for example, the fact that we live on the surface of the earth (unlike whales), the fact that we have eyes (unlike worms) and thus can *see* the heavens, the fact that we are so situated that the seasonal positions of heavenly bodies are intricately connected with agriculture—all these facts are clearly connected with the development of astronomy. The fact that those distant creatures would experience nature in ways very different from ourselves means that they can be expected to raise very different sorts of questions. Indeed, the mode of emplacement within nature of alien inquirers might be so different as to focus their attention on entirely different aspects of constituents of the cosmos. If the world is sufficiently complex and multifaceted, they might concentrate upon aspects of their environment that mean nothing to us, with the result that their natural science is oriented in directions very different from ours.[10]

Epistemologists have often said things to the effect that people whose experience of the world is substantially different from our own are bound to conceive of it in very different terms. Sociologists, anthropologists, and linguists talk in much the same terms, and philosophers of science have recently also come to say the same sorts of things. According to Thomas Kuhn, for example, scientists who work within different scientific traditions—and thus operate with different descriptive and explanatory paradigms—actually 'live in different worlds'.[11]

It is (or should be) clear that there is no simple, unique, ideally adequate concept-framework for describing the world. The botanist, horticulturist, landscape gardener, farmer, and painter will operate from diverse cognitive points of view to describe one selfsame vegetable garden. It is merely mythology to think that the phenomena of nature can lend themselves to only one correct style of descriptive and explanatory conceptualizations. There is surely no ideal scientific language that has a privileged status for the characterization of reality. Different sorts of creatures are bound to make use of different conceptual schemes for the representation of their experience. To insist on the ultimate uniqueness of our science is to succumb to 'the myth of the God's-eye view'. Different cognitive perspectives are possible, no one of them more adequate or more correct than any other independently of the aims and purposes of their users.

[10] His anthropological investigations pointed Benjamin Lee Whorf in much this same direction. He wrote, 'The real question is: What do different languages do, not with artificially isolated objects, but with the flowing face of nature in its motion, color, and changing form; with clouds, beaches, and yonder flight of birds? For as goes our segmentation of the face of nature, so goes our physics of the cosmos' ('Language and Logic', in J. B. Carroll (ed.), *Language, Thought, and Reality* (Cambridge, Mass.: MIT Press, 1956), 240–1). Compare also the interesting discussion in Thomas Nagel, 'What is it Like to be a Bat?', in *Mortal Questions* (Cambridge, Mass.: Harvard University Press, 1976).

[11] Thomas Kuhn, *The Structure of Scientific Revolutions* (Chicago: University of Chicago Press, 1962).

Supporting considerations for this position have been advanced from strongly divergent points of view. One example is a *Gedankenexperiment* suggested by Georg Simmel in the last century, which envisaged an entirely different sort of cognitive being: intelligent and actively inquiring creatures (animals, say, or beings from outer space) whose experiential modes are quite different from our own.[12] Their senses respond rather differently to physical influences: they are relatively insensitive, say, to heat and light, but substantially sensitized to various electromagnetic phenomena. Such intelligent creatures, Simmel held, could plausibly be supposed to operate within a largely different framework of empirical concepts and categories; the events and objects of the world of their experience might be quite different from those of our own: their phenomenological predicates, for example, might have altogether variant descriptive domains. In a similar vein, Williams James wrote:

Were we lobsters, or bees, it might be that our organization would have led to our using quite different modes from these [actual ones] of apprehending our experiences. It *might* be too (we cannot dogmatically deny this) that such categories unimaginable by us to-day, would have proved on the whole as serviceable for handling our experiences mentally as those we actually use.[13]

The constitution of alien inquirers—physical, biological, and social—thus emerges as crucial for science. It would be bound to condition the agenda of questions and the instrumentalities for their resolution—to fix what is seen as interesting, important, relevant, and significant. Because it determines what is seen as an appropriate question and what is judged as an admissible solution, the cognitive posture of the inquirers must be expected to play a crucial role in shaping the course of scientific inquiry itself.

Like our own science of the temporally remote future, the science of spatially remote aliens must be presumed to be such that we really could not achieve intellectual access to it on the basis of our own position in the cognitive scheme of things. Just as the technology of a more advanced civilization would be bound to strike us as magic, so its science would be bound to strike us as incomprehensible gibberish—until we had learned it from the ground up. They might (just

---

[12] Georg Simmel, 'Über eine Beziehung der Selektionslehre zur Erkenntnistheorie', *Archiv für systematische Philosophie und Soziologie*, 1 (1895), 34–45 (see pp. 40–1).
[13] William James, *Pragmatism* (New York: Longmans Green, 1907).

barely) be able to *teach* it to us, but they could not *explain* it to us by transposing it into our terms. The most characteristic and significant difference between one conceptual scheme and another arises when the one scheme is committed to something the other does not envisage at all—something that lies outside the conceptual range of the other. A typical case is that of the stance of Cicero's thought-world with regard to questions of quantum electrodynamics. The Romans of classical antiquity did not hold *different* views on these issues; they held no view at all about them. This whole set of relevant considerations remained outside their conceptual repertoire. The diversified history of *our* terrestrial science gives one some minuscule inkling of the vast range of possibilities along these lines.

The science of different civilizations may well, like Galenic and Pasteurian medicine, simply change the subject in key respects so as no longer to talk about the same things, but deal with materials (e.g. humours and bacteria, respectively) of which the other takes no cognizance at all. The difference in regard to conceptual schemes between modern and Galenic medicine is not that the modern physician has a different theory of the operation of the four humours from his Galenic counterpart but that modern medicine has *abandoned* the four humours, and not that the Galenic physician says different things about bacteria and viruses but that he says *nothing* about them.

As long as the fundamental categories of thought about reality— the modes of spatiality and temporality, of structural description, functional connection, and explanatory rationalization—are not seen as necessary features of intelligence as such, but as evolved cognitive adaptations to particular contingently constituted modes of emplacement in and interaction with nature, there will be no reason to expect uniformity. Sociologists of knowledge tell us that even for us humans here on earth, our Western science is but one of many competing ways of conceptualizing the world's processes. And when one turns outward towards space at large, the prospects of diversity become virtually endless. It is a highly problematic contention even that beings constituted as we are and located in an environment such as ours must inevitably describe and explain natural phenomena in the terms found by current science. And with differently constituted beings, the scope for differentiation is amplified enormously. Given intelligent beings with a physical and cognitive nature profoundly different from ours, one simply cannot assert with confidence what the natural science of such creatures would be like. But nevertheless their science would be well attuned to nature: it would have a close fit to reality—to the world of *their* experience as it emerges through the natural and technological instrumentalities at their disposal for the acquisition of information.

7.4. The Evolutionary Aspect

Our particular human conception of the issues of science is something specifically and parochially characteristic of us, because we are physically, perceptually, and cognitively limited and conditioned by our specific situation within nature. For man's capacity to discover those laws of nature has a perfectly natural and straightforward evolutionary explanation. After all, it should not be particularly surprising that men should succeed in acquiring such knowledge. This is something only natural and to be expected because, if we did not succeed in this cognitive venture, we would not be here—or at any rate not as the sorts of intelligent beings we are. The rationale for this is fundamentally Darwinian: rational guidance is necessary for successful action; successful action is crucial for the survival of creatures constituted as we are; accordingly, our survival is indicative of cognitive competence.

This important fact was clearly perceived by C. S. Peirce as early as around a century ago. Peirce saw man's evolutionary adaptation as an evolutionary product that endows his mind with a kind of functional sympathy for the processes of nature.

[M]an's mind has a natural adaptation to imagining correct theories of some kinds, and in particular to [*sic*] correct theories about forces, without some glimmer of which he could not form social ties and consequently could not reproduce his kind. In short, the instincts conducive to assimilation of food, and the instincts conducive to reproduction, must have involved from the beginning certain tendencies to think truly about physics, on the one hand, and about psychics, on the other. It is somehow more than a mere figure of speech to say that nature fecundates the mind of man with ideas which, when those ideas grow up, will resemble their father, Nature.

(*Collected Papers* (1903), v. 591)

For Peirce the validation of man's scientific talent lies in evolution. Under the pressure of evolutionary forces, the mind of man has come to be 'co-natured' with physical reality.[14] Peirce's argument is clearly on the right track. It is no more a miracle that the human mind can understand the world than that the human eye can see it.

Consider the range of questions that arise in this area: How is it that we humans are actually so competent in coping with matters of cognitive complexity? How is it that we possess the intellectual talent to create mathematics, medicine, science, engineering, architecture, literature, and other comparably splendid cognitive disciplines? What explains the immensely penetrating power of our intellectual capacities?

At a level of high generality the answer to such questions is relatively straightforward. Basically, we are so intelligent because this is our place in evolution's scheme of things. Different sorts of creatures have different ecological niches, different specialities that enable them to find their evolutionary way along the corridor of time. Some are highly prolific, some protected by hard shells, some swift of foot, some difficult to spot, some extremely timid. But *Homo sapiens* is different. For the evolutionary instrument of our species is intelligence—with everything that this involves in the way of abilities and versatilities.

Of course it is not all just a matter of fate's lottery happening to bring intelligence our way. Evolution's bio-engineering is the crucial factor. Bees and termites can achieve impressive prodigies of collective effort. But an insect developed under the aegis of evolution could not become as smart as man because the information-processing requirements of its lifestyle are too modest to push its physical resources to the expansion of intelligence. The developments of our brain, of our bodies, and of our lifestyle have proceeded hand in hand.

Intelligence functions as an inherent concomitant of our physical endowment. Our bodies have many more independently movable parts (more degrees of freedom) than do those of most other creatures.[15] This circumstance has significant implications. Suppose a system with n switches, each capable of assuming an on or off

---

[14] For more details regarding Peirce's views on these matters see the author's *Peirce's Philosophy of Science* (Notre Dame: University of Notre Dame Press, 1978).

[15] The human skeleton has some 220 bones, about the same number as a cat when tail bones are excluded. A small monkey has around 120. Of course, what matters for present purposes is *independently* moving parts. This demotes 'thousand leggers' and—thanks to fingers, among other things—takes us out of the cat's league.

position. There are then 2^n states in which the system can find itself. With $n = 3$ there are only 8 system-states, but with n doubling to 6 there are already 64 states. As a body grows more complex and its configuration takes on more degrees of freedom, the range of alternative possible states expands rapidly (exponentially). Merely keeping track of its actual position is already difficult. To plan ahead is more difficult yet. If there are m possible states which the system can now assume, then when it comes to selecting its next position there are also m choices, and for the next two there are $m \times m$ alternatives overall (ignoring unrealizable combinations). So with a two-step planning horizon the 3–state system has 64 alternatives while the 6–state system has 4,096. With a mere doubling of states, the planning problem has become complicated by a factor of 64.

Considerations of this sort render it evident that a vertebrate creature that has a more highly articulated skeleton which equips it with many independently operable bones and bone-complexes, will thereby face vastly greater difficulties in management and manipulation—in what military jargon calls 'command and control'. Versatile behaviour involves more complex supervision. And so, physically more versatile animals have to be smarter simply because they are physically more versatile. The degrees of freedom inherent in variable movement over time are pivotal considerations here. The moment one walks upright and begins to develop the modes of motion that this new posture facilitates—by way of creeping, running, leaping, etc.—one has many more factors of physical movement to manage.

Environmental surveillance is crucial for our human lifestyle because nourishment, comfort, and security are things we need to achieve through action. The complexity of our sophisticated surveillance mechanisms in the context of friend-or-foe identification is an illustration. We can observe at a considerable distance that people are looking at us, discriminating minute differences in eye orientation in this context. The development of our sophisticated senses with their refined discrimination of odours, colours, and sounds is another example. We have to know which features of our environment to heed and which can safely be ignored. The handling of such a volume of information calls for selectivity and for sophisticated processing mechanisms—in short, for intelligence. Not only must our bodies be the right size to support our physical operations and activities, but our brains must be so as well.

We humans are driven to devising greater capabilities for information acquisition and processing by the greater exigencies of the lifestyle of our ecological niche. The complexities of information management and processing pose unrelenting evolutionary demands. To process a large volume of information, nature must fit us out with a large brain. A battleship needs more elaborate mechanisms for guidance and governance than a rowing-boat. A department store needs a more elaborate managerial apparatus than a corner grocery. Operating a sophisticated body requires a sophisticated mind. How one makes one's living also matters: insect-eating and fruit-eating monkeys have heavier brains, for their size, than do leaf-eating ones.[16] The evolution of the human brain is the story of nature's struggles to provide the machinery of information management and operative control needed by creatures of increasing physical versatility. A feedback cycle comes into play—a complex body requires a larger brain for command and control, and a larger brain requires a larger body whose operational efficiency in turn places greater demands on that brain for the managerial functions required to provide for survival and the assurance of a posterity. As can be illustrated by comparing the brain weights of different mammalian species, the growing complexities and versatilities of animal bodies involve a physical lifestyle whose difficulties of information processing and management require increasingly powerful brains.

Here then is the immediate (and rather trivial) answer to our question: we are as intelligent as we are because that is how we have had to evolve to achieve our niche in nature's scheme of things. We are so smart because evolution's bio-engineering needs to provide intelligence for us to achieve and maintain the lifestyle appropriate to our ecological niche.

But there remains the problem of why evolution would take this course? Surely we did not need to be *that* smart to outwit the sabre-toothed tiger or domesticate the sheep. Let us explore this developmental aspect of the matter a little.

The things we have to do to manage our lifestyle must not only be *possible* for us, they must in general be *easy* for us (so easy that most of them can be done unthinkingly and even unconsciously). If our problem-solving resources were frequently strained to the limit, often

---

[16] At any given time in evolutionary history, the then-current herbivores tended to have smaller brains than the contemporary carnivores. See Richard Dawkin, *The Blind Watchmaker* (New York: Norton, 1986), 190.

groaning under the weight of difficulty of the problems that they are called on by nature to solve in the interests of our lifestyle, then we just would not have achieved the sort of place we actually occupy in the world's scheme of things.

For evolution to do its work, the survival problems that creatures confront must by and large be easily manageable by the mechanisms at their disposal. And this fundamental principle holds just as true for cognitive as for biological evolution. If cognitive problem-solving were too difficult for our mental resources, we would not evolve as problem-solving creatures. If we had to go to as great lengths to work out 2 + 2 as to extract the cube root of a number, or if it took us as long to discriminate 3- from 4-sided figures as it takes to discriminate between 296- and 297-sided ones, then these sorts of issues would simply remain outside our intuitive repertoire. The 'average' problems of survival and thriving that are posed by our lifestyle must be of the right level of difficulty for us—that is, they must be relatively easy. And this calls for excess capacity. All the ordinary problems of one's mode of life must be solvable quickly in real time—and with enough idle capacity left over to cope with the unusual.

A brain that is able to do the necessary things when and as needed to sustain the life of a complex and versatile creature will remain underutilized much of the time. To cope during times of peak demand, it will need to have a great deal of excess capacity to spare for other issues at slack times. And so, any brain powerful enough to accomplish those occasionally necessary tasks must have the excess capacity to pursue at most normal times various challenging projects that have nothing whatsoever to do with survival.

These deliberations conspire to resolve the objection that evolution cannot explain our intellectual capacities because we are a lot smarter than evolution demands—that, after all, nature does not quiz us on higher mathematics or theoretical physics. What is being maintained here is not the absurd contention that development of such sophisticated disciplines is somehow an evolutionary requisite but only that the capacities and abilities that make such enterprises possible are evolutionarily advantageous—that evolution equips us with a reserve capacity that makes them possible as a side-benefit.[17]

---

[17] For example, mathematical discovery often anticipates applicative utility in physics. But this should be no more surprising than that earlier inventions in technology facilitate later applications beyond the dreams of their discoverers.

To be sure, evolution is not, in general, over-generous. For example, evolution will not develop creatures whose running speed is vastly greater than what is needed to escape their predators, to catch their prey, or to realize some other such universal-facilitating objective. But intelligence and its works are a clear exception to this general rule, owing to its self-catalyzing nature. With cognitive artefacts as with many physical artefacts, the character of the issues prevents a holding back; when one can do a little with calculation or with information processing, one can in principle do a great deal. Once evolution opens the door to intelligence, it gets the run of the house. When bio-design takes the route of intelligence to secure an evolutionary advantage for a creature, it embarks on a slippery slope. Having started along this road, there is no easy and early stop. For once a species embarks on using intelligence as its instrument for coping with nature, then the pressure of species-internal competition enters as a hot-house forcing process. Intelligence itself becomes a goad to further development simply because intelligence is, as it were, developmentally self-energizing.

The result of such deliberations is straightforward. Intelligence is the evolutionary speciality of *Homo sapiens*. If we were markedly less smart than we in fact are, we would not have been able to survive—or rather, more accurately, we would not have been able to develop into the sort of creatures we have become. Intelligence constitutes the characteristic speciality that provides the comparative advantage that has enabled our species to make its evolutionary way into this world's scheme of things. We are so smart because this is necessary for *us* to be here at all as the sort of creatures we have been able to become. For if we were not so intelligent, we would not be here as the sort of creatures we are. We have all those splendid intellectual capacities because we require them in order to be ourselves.

And in the course of deploying our intelligence to grapple with the complexities of the world about us we arrived ultimately at the project of natural science. Gradually our natural curiosity got the better of us and we began to push the project of inquiry beyond the level of actual need. It is not that we require scientific ability to exist in our evolutionary niche (thank goodness!). Instead, the fact is that what we require for occupying our evolutionary niche is a body of skills that also renders the development of science possible.

Cognitive evolution is doubtless no different from all evolution in consisting of a long series of improbable accidents. But this does not make them any more inexplicable than any other improbable developments that occur in the world. (The fact that one could not have predicted them does not mean that one cannot explain them with the wisdom of *ex post facto* hindsight.[18]) There is no mystery or unintelligibility here. For the key point is that there is a perfectly good explanation—to wit, an *evolutionary* explanation—of our success at discovering laws (and systematizing factual knowledge in general). And this explanation is clearly such that the past successes at issue augur good future prospects.

In sum, then, it is no more a miracle that the human mind can understand the world through its conceptual resources than that the human eye can see it through its physiological resources. The critical step is to recognize that the question, 'Why do our conceptual methods and mechanisms fit the real world with which we interact intellectually?' is to be answered in basically the same way as the question, 'Why do our bodily processes and mechanisms fit the world with which we interact physically?' In neither case can we proceed in terms of purely theoretical grounds of general principle. Both issues are alike to be resolved in essentially evolutionary terms. It is no more surprising that our minds grasp some of nature's ways than it is surprising that our eyes can accommodate some of nature's rays or our stomachs some of nature's food.

All the same, it could be the case that we do well as regards our cognitive adjustment only in the immediate local microenvironment that defines our particular limited ecological niche. The possibility still remains open that we secure our cognitive hold on only a small and peripheral part of a large and impenetrable whole. And so, man's own one-sided contribution to the matter of nature's intelligibility cannot be the whole story regarding the success of science. Nature too must do its part in this fundamentally interactive process.

To clarify this issue we must therefore move on to consider nature's contribution to the bilateral mind/nature relationship.

7.5. Nature's Side

What needs to be explained for present purposes is why mathematics is not merely of *some* utility in understanding the world, but actually

---

[18] Consider the analogy of quantum phenomena such as the radioactive decay of atoms of a heavy element. Here the fact that one cannot predict does not mean one cannot explain the phenomena at issue.

of very *substantial* utility—that its employment can provide intelligent inquirers with an adequate and accurate grasp of nature's ways. We must thus probe more deeply into the issue of nature's amenability to inquiry and its accessibility to the probes of intelligence.

The effective applicability of mathematics to the description of nature undoubtedly owes its existence in part to the fact that we actually devise our mathematics to fit nature through the mediation of experience. However, the fact remains that man is an inquiring being emplaced within nature and forms mathematicized conceptions and beliefs about it on the basis of physical interaction with it in order to achieve a reasonably appropriate grasp of its workings. Thus nature too must do its part: it must be duly benign. Obviously it must permit the evolution of inquiring beings. But that is not enough.

Nature's own contribution to the issue of the mathematical intelligibility of nature must accordingly be the possession of a relatively simple and uniform law structure—one that deploys so uncomplicated a set of regularities that even a community of inquirers possessed of only rather modest capabilities can be expected to achieve a fairly good grasp of it.

But how can one establish that—relative to our suppositions—nature simply *must* have a fairly straightforward law structure? Are there any fundamental reasons why the world that we investigate by the use of our mathematically informed intelligence should operate on relatively simple principles that are readily amenable to mathematical characterization? There are indeed. For a world in which intelligence emerges by anything like a standard evolutionary process is a realm that has to be pervaded by regularities and periodicities in the organism–nature interaction that produces and perpetuates organic species. And this means that nature must be co-operative in a certain very particular way—it must be stable enough, regular enough, and structured enough for there to be appropriate responses to natural events that can be learned by creatures. If such appropriate responses are to develop, nature must provide suitable stimuli in a duly structured way. Nature must thus present us with an environment that affords sufficiently stable patterns to make coherent experience possible, enabling us to derive appropriate information from our structured interactions with the environment. An organically viable environment—to say nothing of a knowable one—must incorporate experientiable structures. There must be regular patterns of occurrence in nature that even simple, single-celled creatures can embody in their make-up and reflect in their *modus operandi*. Even the humblest organisms, snails, say, and even algae, must so operate that certain *types of stimuli* (patterns of recurrently discernible impacts) call forth appropriately corresponding types of response—that such organisms can detect a structured pattern in their natural environment and react to it in a way that proves to their advantage in evolutionary terms. Even its simplest creatures can maintain themselves in existence only by swimming in a sea of detectable regularities of a sort that will be readily accessible to intelligence. Accordingly, a world in which any form of intelligence evolves will have to be a world that is congenial to mathematics, the abstract and systematic theory of structure-in-general.

The development of life and, thereafter, of intelligence in the world may or may not be inevitable; the emergence of intelligent creatures on the world's stage may or may not be surprising in itself and as such. But once they are there, and once we realize that they got there thanks to evolutionary processes, it can no longer be seen as surprising that their efforts at characterizing the world in mathematical terms should be substantially successful. The crux of it is that a world in which intelligent creatures emerge through the operation of evolutionary processes must be a mathematically intelligible world.

Moreover, intelligence must give an evolutionary edge to its possessors. The world must encapsulate straightforwardly learnable patterns and periodicites of occurrence in its operations—relatively simple laws. The existence of such learnable 'structures' of stability in natural occurrence means that there must be *some* useful role for mathematics, which, after all, is the science of structure. And so we may conclude that a world in which intelligence can develop by evolutionary processes *must* also—on this basis—be a world amenable to understanding in mathematical terms.[19] Such a world must be one in which such beings will find considerable ammunition in endeavouring to understand the world. Galileo came close when he wrote in his *Dialogues* that: 'Nature initially arranged things her *own* way and subsequently so constructed the human intellect as to be able to understand her.'[20]

---

[19] Conversations with Gerald Massey have helped in clarifying this part of the argument.
[20] Galileo Galilei, *Dialogo* 2, *Le Opere di Galileo Galilei*, Edizione Nationale (20 vols.; Florence, 1890–1909), vii. 298. (I owe this reference to Jürgen Mittelstrass.) Recall also his

The apparent success of human mathematics in characterizing nature is thus not at all amazing. It may or may not call for wonder that we have a world in which intelligent creatures should evolve at all, but once they have safely arrived on the scene through evolutionary means, that they should be able to achieve success in the project of understanding nature in mathematical terms is only to be expected. An intelligence-containing world whose intelligent creatures came by this attribute through evolutionary means must be substantially intelligible in mathematical terms. On this line of deliberation, then, nature admits to mathematical depiction not just because it has laws (is a cosmos), but because it has relatively simple laws, and those relatively simple laws must be there because if they were not, then nature just could not afford a potential environment for intelligent life.

The strictly hypothetical and conditional character of this general line of reasoning must be recognized. It does not maintain that by virtue of some sort of transcendental necessity the world has to be simple enough for its mode of operation to admit of elegant mathematical representation. Rather, what it maintains is the purely conditional thesis that *if* intelligent creatures are going to emerge in the world by evolutionary processes, *then* the world must be mathematophile, with various of its processes amenable to mathematical representation.

It must be stressed, however, that this conditional fact is quite sufficient for present purposes. For the question we face is why we intelligent creatures present on the world's stage should be able to understand its operations in terms of our mathematics. The conditional story at issue fully suffices to accomplish this particular job.

7.6. Synthesis

Let us review the course of present reasoning. The overall question of the intelligibility of nature has two sides: (1) Why is mind so well attuned to nature? (2) Why is nature so well attuned to mind? The preceding discussion has suggested that the answers to these questions are not all that complicated—at least at the level of schematic

observation in the *Assayer* about the book of nature being written in mathematical characters.

essentials. The crux is simply this: mind must be attuned to nature since intelligence is a generalized guide to conduct that has evolved as a natural product of nature's operations. And nature must be accessible to mind if intelligence manages to evolve within nature by a specifically evolutionary route.

For nature to be intelligible, then, there must be an alignment that requires co-operation on both sides. The analogy of cryptanalysis is suggestive. If *A* is to break *B*'s code, there must be due reciprocal alignment. If *A*'s methods are too crude, too hit and miss, he can get nowhere. But even if *A* is quite intelligent and resourceful, his efforts cannot succeed if *B*'s procedures are simply beyond his powers. (The cryptanalysts of the seventeenth century, clever though they were, could get absolutely nowhere in applying their investigative instrumentalities to a high-level naval code of World War II vintage.) Analogously, if mind and nature were too far out of alignment—if mind were too 'unintelligent' for the complexities of nature or nature too complex for the capacities of mind—the two just could not get into step. It would be like trying to rewrite Shakespeare in a pidgin English with a 500-word vocabulary, or like trying to monitor the workings of a system containing ten degrees of freedom by using a cognitive mechanism capable of keeping track of only four of them. If something like this were the case, mind could not accomplish its evolutionary mission. The interests of survival would have been better served by an alignment process that does not take the cognitive route.

7.7. Implications

The possibility of a mathematical science of nature is accordingly to be explained by the fact that, in the light of evolution, intelligence and intelligibility must stand in mutual co-ordination. The following three points are paramount here:

1. Intelligence evolves within a nature that provides for life because it affords living creatures a good way of coming to terms with the world.

2. Once intelligent creatures evolve, their cognitive efforts are likely to have some degree of adequacy because evolutionary pressures align them with nature's ways.

3. It should not be surprising that this alignment eventually produces a substantially effective mathematical physics, because the structure of the operations of a nature that engenders intelligence by an evolutionary route is bound to be relatively regular.

There may indeed be mysteries in this general area. (Such questions as, 'Why should it be that *life* evolves in the world?' and—even more fundamentally—'Why should it be that the world exists at all?' may plausibly be proposed as candidates.) But be that as it may, the presently deliberated issue of why nature is intelligible to us, and why this intelligibility should incorporate a mathematically articulable physics, does not qualify as all that mysterious, let alone miraculous. No doubt, this general account is highly schematic and requires a great deal of elaboration and amplification. A long and complex tale must be told about physical and cognitive evolution to fill in the details needed to put such an account into a properly compelling form. But there is surely good reason to hope and expect that a tale of this sort can ultimately be told. And this is the pivotal point. Even if one has doubts about the particular outlines of the evolutionary story we have sketched, the fact remains that *some such story* can provide a perfectly workable answer to the question of why nature's ways are intelligible to *Homo sapiens* in terms of our mathematical instrumentalities. The mere fact that such an account is in principle possible shows that the issue need not be painted in the black on black of impenetrable mystery.

The existence of the world may be a mystery, but given that it does exist and thereby has certain features (as the product of the operation of evolutionary processes) the possession of other features (mathematical intelligibility) will thereby become correlatively explicable. And so, there is simply no need to join Einstein, Schroedinger, *et al.*, in considering the intelligibility of nature as a miracle or a mystery that passes all human understanding. If we are willing to learn from science itself how nature operates and how man goes about conducting his inquiries into its workings, then we should be able increasingly to remove the shadow of incomprehension from the problem of how it is that a being of *this* sort, probing an environment of *that* type, and doing so by means of those evolutionarily developed cognitive and physical instrumentalities, manages to arrive at a relatively workable account of how things work in the world. We should eventually be able to see it as only plausible and to be expected that inquiring beings should emerge in nature and get themselves into a position to make a relatively good job of coming to comprehend it. We can thus *look to science itself* for the materials that enable us to understand how natural science is possible. And there is no good reason to expect that it will let us down in this regard.

But does such a scientific explanation of the success of science not explain too much? Will its account of the pervasiveness of mathematical exactness in science not lead to the (obviously problematic) consequence that 'science gets it right'—a result that would fly in the face of our historical experience of science's fallibilism? By no means! It is fortunate (and evolutionarily most relevant) that we are so positioned within nature that many 'wrong' paths lead to the 'right' destination—that flawed means often lead us to cognitively satisfactory ends. If nature were a combination lock where we simply had to get it right—and *exactly* right—to achieve success in implementing our beliefs, then we just would not be here. Evolution is not an argument that speaks unequivocally for the adequacy of our cognitive efforts. On the contrary, properly construed it is an indicator of our capacity to err and get away with it. Our achievements can be (and doubtless are) the product of an evolutionary alignment of inquirers to the environment that they investigate—an alignment that can stop well short of a perfect fit simply because that world must, in the evolutionary nature of things, constitute a highly error-tolerant environment.

The success of science should be understood somewhat by analogy with the success of the man who, seeking to slake his thirst, drank white grape juice, mistaking it for lemonade. It is not that he was roughly right—that grape juice is 'approximately' lemonade. It is just that his beliefs are not wrong in ways that lead to his being baffled in his present purposes. Equally, it is not that our science as we now have it gets everything right. Rather, it is that such defects as there are simply do not matter for the issues currently in hand. The massive successes of our science are thus not to be explained on the basis of its actually getting at the real truth, but in terms of it being the work of a cognitive being who operates within an error-tolerant environment—a world-setting where applicative and cognitive success will attend even theories that are substantially off the mark. The applicative efficacy of science undoubtedly requires *some* degree of alignment between our world-picture and the world's actual arrangements, but not perfection—only sufficiency to yield the particular successes at issue. Here as elsewhere evolution operates in such a way that the predator need outrun its prey by only a small margin. We arrive at the picture of nature as an error-tolerant system. For consider the hypothetical situation of a species of belief-guided creatures living in an environment that invariably exacts a great penalty for getting it wrong. Whenever the creature makes the smallest mistake—the least little cognitive misstep—bang, it's dead! Our hypothesis is not viable: any such creature would have been eliminated long ago. It could not even manage to survive and reproduce long enough to learn about its environment by trial and error. If the world is to be a home for intelligent beings who develop in it through evolution, then it has to be benign. If *seeming* success in intellectually governed operations could not attend even substantially erroneous beliefs, then we cognizing beings who have to learn by experience—by trial and error—just could not have made our evolutionary way along the corridor of time as the sort of (intelligent) creatures that we are. If nature were not error-forgiving, a process of evolutionary trial and error could not work and intelligent organisms could not emerge at all. It follows that intelligence and the science it devises must pay off in terms of applicative success—irrespective of whether it manages to get things substantially right or not. In the circumstances, we cannot help labouring under the impression that our science is rather successful. There is not—or should not be—any mystery about it.[21]

---

[21] Some of the issues of this chapter are also explored in the author's *A Useful Inheritance* (Savage, Md.: Rowman Littlefield, 1990), and in *The Riddle of Existence* (Lanham, Md.: University Press of America, 1984).

8

Optimalism and Axiological Metaphysics

SYNOPSIS

(1) The Leibnizian problem, 'Why is there anything rather than nothing?' has intrigued and challenged philosophers over the years. (2) Here Leibniz's own idea of an axiological explanation is worth exploring. (3) It can be defended against various objections. (4) In particular, the question of how value can have explanatory efficacy can be resolved. (5) Axiological explanations need not be purposive. (6) They can, moreover, be entirely naturalistic and (7) be developed free of theological involvements. (Appendix) The presently contemplated axiological ontogenesis is something different from the deontological ontogenesis recently propounded by the Canadian philosopher John Leslie.

8.1. The Riddle of Existence

What is perhaps the biggest metaphysical question of them all was put on the agenda of philosophy by G. W. Leibniz: 'Why is there anything at all?' This question is not only difficult to answer but poses difficulties in its very conception. After all, it is—or should be—clear that such questions as 'Why is there anything at all?', 'Why are things-in-general as they actually are?', and 'Why are the laws of nature as they are?' cannot be answered within the standard causal framework. For causal explanations need inputs: they are essentially *transformational* rather than *formational* pure and simple. And so, if we persist in posing the sorts of global questions at issue, we cannot hope to resolve them in orthodox causal terms. For when we ask about *everything* there are no issue-external materials at our disposal for giving a non-circular explanation. Does this mean that such questions are improper and should not be raised at all—that even to inquire into the existence of the entire universe is somehow illegitimate? Not necessarily. For it could be replied that the question does have a perfectly good answer, but one that is not given in the orthodox causal terms that apply to other issues of smaller scale. A more radical strategy is thus called for if rejectionism is to be avoided. And such a strategy exists.

But before turning in this direction, let us consider more closely a rejectionism that holds that it is just a mistake to ask for a causal explanation of existence *per se*; the question should be abandoned as improper—as not representing a legitimate issue. The line of thought in contention here holds that in the light of closer scrutiny the explanatory 'problem' vanishes as meaningless.

Such a dismissal of the problem as illegitimate is generally based on the idea that the question at issue involves an illicit presupposition because it looks to answers of the form '*Z* is the (or an) explanation for the existence of things.' Committed to this response-schema, the question presupposes the thesis, 'There actually is a ground for the existence of things—existence-in-general is the sort of thing that has an explanation.' And this presumption, we are told, is false on the grounds of deep general principles inherent in the logical nature of the case.

Consider the following suggestion along these lines made by C. G. Hempel:

Why is there anything at all, rather than nothing? . . . But what kind of an answer could be appropriate? What seems to be wanted is an explanatory account which does not assume the existence of something or other. But such an account, I would submit, is a logical impossibility. For generally, the question 'Why is it the case that *A*?' is answered by 'Because *B* is the case' . . . [A]*n answer to our riddle which made no assumptions about the existence of anything cannot possibly provide adequate grounds. . . .* The riddle has been constructed in a manner that makes an answer logically impossible.[1]

However, this apparently plausible line of argumentation has shortcomings, the most serious of which is that it fails to distinguish appropriately between the existence of things on the one hand and the obtaining of facts on the other,[2] and supplementarily also

---

[1] Carl G. Hempel, 'Science Unlimited', *The Annals of the Japan Association for Philosophy of Science*, 14 (1973), 187–202 (see p. 200). My italics.
[2] Note too that the question of the existence of facts is a horse of a very different colour from that of the existence of *things*. There being no things is undoubtedly a possible

between specifically substantival facts regarding *existing things,* and non-substantival facts regarding *states of affairs* that are bound to particular things. (Unlike saying that the sun is hot, saying that the day is hot does not ascribe that heat to an object of some sort.) We are confronted here with a principle of hypostatization to the effect that the reason for anything must ultimately always inhere in the properties of things. And at this point we come to a prejudice as deep-rooted as any in Western philosophy: the idea that things can only originate from things, that nothing can come from nothing (*ex nihilo nihil fit*) in the sense that no *thing* can emerge from an amorphously thingless condition.[3] Now, this somewhat ambitious principle is perfectly unproblematic when construed as saying that if the existence of something real has a correct explanation at all, then this explanation must pivot on something that is really and truly so. Clearly, we cannot explain one *fact* without invoking other *facts* to do the explaining. But the principle becomes highly problematic when construed in the manner of the precept that 'things must come from things', that substances must inevitably be invoked to explain the existence of substances. For we then become committed to the thesis that everything in nature has an efficient cause in some other natural thing that is its causal source, its reason for being.

This stance is implicit in Hempel's argument. And it is explicit in much of the philosophical tradition. Hume, for one, insists that there is no feasible way in which an existential conclusion can be obtained from non-existential premisses.[4] And the principle is also supported by philosophers of a very different ilk on the other side of the channel—including Leibniz himself, who writes: 'The sufficient reason [of contingent existence] ... *must be outside this series of contingent things, and must reside in a substance which is the cause of this series.*'[5] Such a view amounts to a thesis of genetic homogeneity that

situation, there being no *facts* is not (since if the situation were realized, this would itself constitute a fact).

[3] Aristotle taught that every change must emanate from a 'mover', i.e. a substance whose machinations provide the cause of change. This commitment to causal reification is at work in much of the history of Western thought. That its pervasiveness is manifest at virtually every juncture is clear from William Lane Craig's interesting study of *The Cosmological Argument from Plato to Leibniz* (London: Macmillan, 1980).

[4] David Hume, *Dialogues Concerning Natural Religion,* ed. N. K. Smith (London: Longmans, Green, 1922), 189.

[5] G. W. Leibniz, 'Principles of Nature and of Grace', sect. 8, italics supplied. Compare St Thomas: 'Of necessity, therefore, anything that in process of change is being changed by

says (by analogy with the old but now rather obsolete principle that 'life must come from life') that 'things must come from things', or 'stuff must come from stuff', or 'substance must come from substance'. What, after all, could be more plausible than the precept that only real (*existing*) causes can have real (*existing*) effects?

But despite its historic stature, this principle has its problems. It presupposes that there must be a type-homogeneity between cause and effect on the lines of the ancient Greek principle that 'like must come from like'. And this highly dubious principle of genetic homogeneity has taken hard knocks in the course of modern science which has, to all appearances, given up on the 'effect must resemble cause' idea. Matter can come from energy, and living organisms from complexes of inorganic molecules. If the principle fails with matter and life, need it hold for substance as such? The claim that it does so would need a very cogent defence. And none has been forthcoming to date.

Is it indeed true that only *things* can engender things? Why need a ground of change always inhere in a *thing* rather than in a non-substantival 'condition of things-in-general'? Must substance inevitably arise from *substance*? Even to state such a principle clearly is in effect to challenge its credentials. What is to say that substance cannot emerge from pure process? Why must the explanation of facts rest in the operation *of things*? To be sure, fact-explanations must have inputs (*all* explanations must). Facts must root in facts. But why thing-existential ones? A highly problematic bit of metaphysics is involved here. Dogmas about explanatory homogeneity aside, there is no discernible reason why an existential fact cannot be grounded in non-existential ones, and why the existence of substantial *things* cannot be explained on the basis of some non-substantival circumstance or principle whose operations can constrain existence in something of the way in which equations can constrain non-zero solutions. Once we give up the principle of genetic homogeneity and abandon the idea that existing things must originate in existing things, we remove the key prop of the idea that asking for an explanation of things in general is a logically inappropriate demand. The footing of the rejectionist approach is gravely undermined.

something else.' (*Summa Theologiae*, Iq. 2 a.3). The idea that only substances can produce changes goes back to Thomas's master, Aristotle. In Plato and the Presocratics, the causal efficacy of *principles* is recognized (e.g. the love and strife of Empedocles).

There are also further routes to rejectionism. One of them turns on the doctrine of Kant's *Antinomy* that it is illegitimate to try to account for the phenomenal universe as a whole (the entire *Erscheinungswelt*). Explanation on this view is inherently partitive: phenomena can only be accounted for in terms of other particular phenomena, so that it is in principle improper to ask for an account of phenomena-as-a-whole. The very idea of an explanatory science of nature-as-a-whole is illegitimate. Yet this view is deeply problematic. To all intents and purposes, science strives to explain the age of the universe-as-a-whole, its structure, its volume, its laws, its composition, etc. Why not then its *existence* as well? The decree that explanatory discussion in general is by nature necessarily partial and incapable of dealing with the whole lacks plausibility. It seems a mere device for side-stepping embarrassingly difficult questions.

In the end, then, it must be acknowledged that rejectionism is not a particularly appealing doctrine. For its alternatives have the significant merit of retaining for rational inquiry and investigation a question that would otherwise be abandoned. After all, the question of 'the reason why' behind existence is surely important. If there is any possibility of getting an adequate answer—by hook or by crook—it seems reasonable that we would very much like to have it. There is nothing patently meaningless or clearly improper about this riddle of existence. And it does not seem to rest in any obvious way on any particularly problematic presupposition—apart from the epistemically optimistic yet methodologically inevitable idea that there are always reasons why things are as they are (the Principle of Sufficient Reason). To dismiss the question as improper or illegitimate is fruitless; try as we will to put it away, it comes back to haunt us.[6] And yet, extraordinary problems are likely to require extraordinary solutions.

8.2. Optimalism and Evaluative Metaphysics

From its earliest days, metaphysics has been understood also to include 'axiology', the evaluative and normative assessment of the things that exist. As early as Aristotle the aim of the enterprise was

---

[6] For criticisms of ways of avoiding the question, 'Why is there something rather than nothing?' see William Rowe, *The Cosmological Argument* (Princeton: Princeton University Press, 1975), ch. 3. Cf. also Donald R. Burrill (ed.), *The Cosmological Argument* (Garden City, NY: Anchor Books, 1967), esp. 'The Cosmological Argument' by Paul Edwards.

not just to describe or characterize, but to grade (appraise, rank) matters in point of their inherent value. Such metaphysical evaluation has two cardinal features: (1) it is genuine evaluation that involves some authentic concept of greater or lesser value and (2) the mode of value involved is *sui generis* and thus not ethical, aesthetic, utilitarian, etc. Accordingly, it evaluates types of things or conditions of things existing in nature (not acts or artefacts) with a view to their intrinsic merit (not simply their 'value-*for*' man or anything else). The very possibility of this axiological enterprise accordingly rests on the acceptance of distinctly metaphysical values—as opposed to ethical (right/wrong), aesthetic (beautiful/ ugly), or practical (useful/useless) ones.

The paternity of evaluative metaphysics in philosophical practice can unhesitatingly be laid at Plato's door, but as a conscious and deliberate philosophical method it can be ascribed to Aristotle. In the *Physics* and the *De Anima* we find him at work not merely at classifying the kinds of things there are in the world, but in ranking and grading them in terms of relative evaluations. Above all, Aristotle's preoccupation in the *Metaphysics* with the ranking schematism of prior/posterior—for which see especially ch. 11 of Bk. 5 (Delta), and ch. 8 of Bk. 9 (Theta)—is indicative of his far-reaching concern with the evaluative dimension of metaphysical inquiry.[7] It was thus a sound insight into the thought-framework of the great Stagirite that led the anti-Aristotelian writers of the Renaissance, and later preeminently Descartes and Spinoza, to attack the Platonic/Aristotelian conception of the embodiment of value in natural and the modern logical positivist opponents of metaphysics to attach the stigma of illegitimacy to all evaluative disciplines. Nevertheless, despite such attacks, evaluative metaphysics has continued as an ongoing part of the Western philosophical tradition as continued by such thinkers as Leibniz, Kant, Hegel, and Whitehead, all of whom envision will-systems where some things have greater value than others.

A prime example of this methodological approach in recent philosophy is G. E. Moore's *Principia Ethica*.[8] For Moore taught

---

[7] His willingness to subscribe to teleological/axiological explanation is clearly attested by his account of the rationale of the continuity of organic existence: 'For since some existing things are eternal . . . while others are capable both of being and of not being, and since the good . . . is always accordingly to its own nature a cause of the better in things . . . for these reasons there is generation of animals' (*De Gener. Animalium,* 731^{b}24–31).

[8] (Cambridge: University of Cambridge Press, 1903). See in particular §§50, 55, 57, 112–13.

that the realm of ethical values is not self-contained but rather roots in a manifold of metaphysical values. His celebrated 'method of absolute isolation' invites us to make comparative evaluations of two hypothetical worlds supposed to be alike in all relevant respects except that in one of them some factor is exhibited which is lacking in the other. Thus Moore argues for the intrinsic value of natural beauty (i.e. its value even apart from human contemplation) by the argument:

[A hypothetical] beautiful world would be better still, if there were human beings in it to contemplate and enjoy its beauty. But that admission makes nothing against my point. If it be once admitted that the beautiful world in itself is better than the ugly, then it follows, that however many beings may enjoy it, and however much better their enjoyment may be than it is itself, yet its mere existence adds something to the goodness of the whole: it is not only a means to our end, but also itself a part thereof. (ibid. §50)

To espouse the project of evaluative metaphysics is thus to give Moore the right as against Henry Sidgwick's thesis that: 'If we consider carefully such permanent results as are commonly judged to be good, other than qualities of human beings, we find nothing that, on reflection, appears to possess this quality of goodness out of relation to human existence, or at least to some [presumably animal] consciousness or feeling.'[9] (There is of course the trivial fact if 'we' do the considering, 'we' do the evaluating as well. The point to be borne in mind, however, is that this need not be done from a humanly parochial let alone an idiosyncratically personal, and 'subjective' standpoint.) Sidgwick to the contrary notwithstanding, man is neither the measure nor necessarily even the measurer of all things in the evaluative domain.

Moore was well aware of the salient difference which, despite some kinship, obtains between standard ethics on the one hand and evaluative metaphysics on the other, recognizing the *sui generis* character of the latter enterprise:

By combining the results of Ethics as to what would be good or bad, with the conclusions of metaphysics, as to what kinds of things there are in the Universe, we get a means of answering the question whether the Universe is, on the whole, good or bad, and how good or bad, compared with what it

[9] Henry Sidgwick, *Methods of Ethics* (London and New York: Macmillan, 1874), bk. I, ch. ix, §4.

might be: a sort of question which has in fact been much discussed by many philosophers.[10]

Such an axiological position does not (as with Sidgwick) see metaphysical evaluation as rooted in ethics but insists on the very reverse relationship. For if 'maximize value!' is indeed a metaphysically grounded maxim of impersonal rationality, and ethical conduct is, by its very nature, of greater value than its contraries, then ethics will ultimately be predicated upon evaluative metaphysics.

In the present discussion, however, it will not be ethics that concerns us but ontology, and the present deliberations will accordingly focus on exploring the role of value in the explanation of existence. The governing idea is to consider the prospect of giving a Leibnizian answer to that Leibnizian question, contemplating the prospect that things exist—and exist as they do—because that is for the best. Can such an optimalism be developed in a way that is at all plausible?

8.3. Axiological Explanation: How Optimalism Works

Accustomed as we are to explanations in the mode of efficient causality, the idea of an axiological explanation of existence on the basis of an evaluative optimalism has a somewhat strange and unfamiliar air about it. Let us consider more closely how it is supposed to work.

The approach rests on adopting what might be called an *axiogenetic optimality principle* to the effect that value represents a decisive advantage in regard to realization in that in the virtual competition for existence among alternatives it is the comparatively best that is bound to prevail.[11] Accordingly, whenever there is a plurality of alternative possibilities competing for realization in point of truth or of existence the (or an) optimal possibility wins out. (An alternative is *optimal* when no better one exists, although it can have equals.) The result is that things exist, and exist as they do, because this is for the (metaphysical) best.

---

[10] *Some Main Problems of Philosophy* (London: Allen & Unwin, 1953), 40 (Collier paperback edn.).
[11] The prime spokesman for this line of thought within the Western philosophical tradition was G. W. Leibniz. A present-day exponent is John Leslie. (See the Appendix to this chapter.) See also N. Rescher, *The Riddle of Existence* (Lanham, Md.: University Press of America, 1984).

It may be a complicated matter to appraise from a metaphysical/ ontological standpoint that condition X is better (inherently more meritorious) than condition Y. But, so optimalism maintains, once this evaluative hurdle is overcome the question 'Why should it be that X rather than Y exists?' is automatically settled by this very fact via the ramifications of optimality. In sum, a Law of Optimality prevails; value (of a suitable—as yet unspecified—sort) so functions in its existential impetus that it lies in the nature of things for (one of) the best of available alternatives to be realized.[12]

But why should it be that optimalism obtains? What sort of plausible argument can be given on this position's behalf? Why should what is for the best exist? The answer to these questions lies in the very nature of the principle itself. It is self-substantiating, seeing it is automatically for the best that the best alternative should exist rather than an inferior rival. But this is just one of its assets;[13] it also offers significant systemic advantages. For of the various plausible existential principles, it transpires—in the end—that it is optimalism that offers the best available alternative.

The principle being, as it were, self-explanatory, it turns out that to ask for a different sort of explanation would be inappropriate. We must expect that any ultimate principle should explain itself and cannot, in the very nature of things, admit of an external explanation in terms of something altogether different. And the impetus to realization inherent in authentic value lies in the very nature of value itself. A rational person would not favour the inferior alternative; and there is no reason to think that a rational reality would do so either.

Certainly one could ask, 'But why should it be that reality is rational?' But this is a problematic proceeding. For to ask this question is to ask for a reason. It is *already* to presume or presuppose the rationality of things, taking the stance that what is so is and must be so for a reason. Once one poses the question 'But why should it be that nature has the feature F?' it is already too late to raise the issue of nature's rationality. In advancing that question the matter at issue has already been tacitly conceded. Anyone who troubles to ask for a

---

[12] To make this work out, the value of a disjunction-alternative has to be fixed at the value of its optimal member, lest the disjunctive 'bundling' of a good alternative with inferior rivals so operates as to eliminate it from competition.

[13] Other principles can also be self-substantiating, seeing that, e.g., the Principle of Pessimism (that the worst of possible alternatives is realized) also has this feature.

reason why nature should have a certain feature is thereby proceeding within a framework of thought where nature's rationality—the amenability of its features to rational explanation—is already presumed.

Yet what is to be the status of a Law of Optimality to the effect that 'whatever possibility is for the best is *ipso facto* the possibility that is actualized'? It is certainly not a logico-conceptually *necessary* truth; from the angle of theoretical logic it has to be seen as a contingent fact—albeit one not about nature as such, but rather one about the manifold of *real* possibility that underlies it. In so far as necessary at all it obtains as a matter of ontological rather than logico-conceptual necessity, while the realm of possibility as a whole is presumably constituted by considerations of logico-metaphysical necessity alone.[14] But the division of this realm into real versus merely speculative possibilities can hinge on contingent considerations: there can be logically contingent laws of possibility even as there are logically contingent laws of nature (i.e. of reality). But if it is contingent then surely it must itself rest on some further explanation? Granted. It itself presumably has an explanation, seeing that one can and should maintain the Leibnizian Principle of Sufficient Reason to the effect that for every contingent fact there is a reason why it is so rather than otherwise. But there is no decisive reason why that explanation has to be deeper and different—that is, no decisive reason why the prospect of *self-explanation* has to be excluded at this fundamental level.[15] After all, we cannot go on putting the explanatory elephant on the back of the tortoise on the back of the alligator ad infinitum: as Aristotle already saw, the explanatory regress has to stop somewhere at a final theory—one that is literally self-explanatory.

What better candidate could there be than the Law of Optimality itself, with the result that the division between real and merely theoretical possibilities is as it is (i.e. value-based) because that itself is for the best? The reasoning at issue proceeds as follows:

[14] The operative perspective envisions a threefold order of necessity/possibility: the logico-conceptual, the ontological or proto-physical, and the physical. It accordingly resists the positivistic tendency of the times to dismiss or ignore that second, intermediate order of considerations. And this is only to be expected since people nowadays tend to see this intermediate realm as predicated in value considerations, a theme that is anathema to present-day scientism.

[15] After all, there is no reason of logico-theoretical principle why propositions cannot be self-certifying. Nothing vicious need be involved in self-substantiation. Think of 'Some statements are true,' or 'This statement stakes a particular rather than a universal claim.'

- The prevailing world order is the best that *can* be actualized—i.e. the best that it is possible to realize.
- The best possible order exists because that is for the best.

Therefore: The prevailing world order exists.

What is self-explanatory here is not the existence of the world (whose explanation after all proceeds from this entire account). It is, rather, the principle of optimality reflected in the second premiss that is self-explanatory—the fact that the best possible order exists. For this fact is part and parcel of the optimal order whose obtaining it validates. The principle being, as it were, self-explanatory. And to ask for a different sort of explanation would be inappropriate. We must expect that any ultimate principle must explain itself and cannot, in the very nature of things, admit of an external explanation in terms of something altogether different. The impetus to realization inherent in authentic value lies in the very nature of value itself. A rational person would not favour the inferior alternative; and a rational reality cannot do so either.

To be sure, the law's operation here presupposes a manifold of suitable value parameters, invoking certain physically relevant features (symmetry, economy, or the like) as merit-manifesting factors. The optimization at issue is—and should be—geared to a scientifically reputable theory of some suitable kind, co-ordinate with a complex of physically relevant factors of a suitable kind. After all, many a possible world will maximize a value of *some* sort (confusion and nastiness included). It is its (presumed) gearing to a positive value which like economy or elegance is plausibly identifiable as physically relevant—contingently identifiable as such subject to scientific inquiry—that establishes optimalism as a reasonable proposition and ultimately prevents the thesis 'optimalism obtains because that's for the best' from declining into vacuity.

Ontological optimalism is closely related to optimism. The optimist holds that 'Whatever exists is for the best', the optimalist maintains the converse, that 'Whatever is for the best exists'. But at least when we are dealing with exclusive and exhaustive alternatives the two theses come to the same thing. For if one of the alternatives A, $A_1, \ldots A_n$ must be the case, then if what is realized is for the best it follows automatically that the best is realized.

Optimalism has many theoretical advantages. Here is just one of them. It is conceivable, one might contend, that the *existence* of the world (i.e. of *a* world) is a necessary fact while nevertheless its *nature* (i.e. of *which* world) is contingent. And this would mean that separate and potentially different answers would have to be provided for the questions, 'Why is there anything at all?' and 'Why is the character of existence as is—why is it that this particular world exists?' However, an axiogenetic approach enjoys the advantage of rational economy in that it proceeds uniformly here. It provides a single uniform rationale for both answers—namely that 'this is for the best'. It accordingly also enjoys the significant merit of providing for the rational economy of explanatory principles.

But is not optimalism merely a version of wishful thinking? Not necessarily. For even as in personal life what is best for us is all too often not at all what we individuals want, so in metaphysics what is abstractly for the best is very unlikely to bear any close relationship to what we would want to have if we humans could have things our way.

However, a threatening difficulty seems to arise in the form of a possibility range that is evaluatively 'topless'—that is, which does not have some alternatives that are optimal in the sense of not being bettered by any other.[16] In such a range each alternative is surpassed by yet another that is better. And so on optimalistic principles it would transpire that there are no real possibilities at all. Within *such* a range there is no optimum and thus no possibility of actualization. Here optimalism must take the bull by the horns. In so far as situations can be imagined which—like that of a topless infinite alternative spectrum—could raise difficulties for the theory, it could and should simply be seen as part and parcel of optimalism to assert that such situations cannot actually arise: that a reality that is benign all the way through is thereby such as to exclude such a problematic situation. As optimalism sees it, the very fact that toplessness conflicts with optimalism excludes it from the range of real possibilities.

But what if there is a *plurality* of perfection-contributory features so interrelated that more of the one demands less of the other? Here it would result that nothing is straightforwardly best. This may be so, but matters need not be straightforward. In such cases one can—and should—resort to a function of combination that allows for the interaction of those different value parameters. For example, with

---

[16] Leibniz saw the existence of the actual world as itself affording a decisive argument against toplessness since existence could not be realized in a realm of topless meritoriousness, since a benevolent creator would be effectively paralysed.

two operative value-making factors, say cheapness (that is, inverse acquisition cost) and durability in the case of a 100–watt light bulb, one will use the ratio (cost of purchase):(hours of usability) or equally cost/hour of service as a measure of merit. This possibilizes the reduction of the multifactor case to the situation of a single compound and complex factor so that optimization is once again possible. And that this is possible is guaranteed by optimalism itself; it is part and parcel of the best possible order of things that optimalism should be operable within it.

But—really!—how can sensible people possibly embrace the conception that the inherently best alternative is thereby automatically the actual (true) one. Does not the world's all too evident imperfection stand decisively in the way here?

The matter is not all that simple, however. For the issue is going to pivot on the question of what 'inherently best' means. If it means best from that angle of your desires, or of my interests, or even of the advantage of *Homo sapiens* in general, then clearly the thesis loses its strong appeal. For such plausibility that 'best' should be construed as looking to the condition of existence-as-a-whole rather than one particular privileged individual or group. Optimality in this context is clearly not going to be a matter of the affective welfare or standard of living of some particular sector of existence; it is going to have to be a metaphysical good of some synoptic and rather abstract sort that looks to the condition of the whole. The optimalist certainly need not simply shut his eyes to the world's all too evident parochially considered imperfections. There is, in fact, a point of view from which optimalism is a position that is not so much optimistic as deeply pessimistic. For it holds that even the best of possible arrangements is bound to exhibit very real imperfections from the angle of any narrowly parochial concerns or interests.

8.4. The Problem of How Value can have Explanatory Efficacy: Overcoming Some Objections

A seeming obstacle to optimalism looms in the question, 'But how can value possibly exert a causally productive influence?' And the answer to this good question is that it does not. What value conditions do is not to create anything (i.e. productively engender its realization). Their *modus operandi* is not causal but modal: their role is to block or preclude certain theoretically conceivable possibilities from realizability. They serve an entirely restrictive function and only manage to preclude certain theoretical possibilities from qualifying as ontological (potentially achievable) possibilities. At this stage we contemplate a tripartite hierarchy of (increasingly substantive) possibilities: logical, ontological, and physical subject to the control of logic, of axiology, and of physics, respectively. It is thus at the middle level of ontological possibilities that axiology does its work. The operative impetus of optimality does not express itself by way of causality in the realm of the real but rather by way of a determination in the realm of the genuinely possible—that is, of the metaphysically rather than logically possible. And this metaphysical possibility should be seen as constraining the most fundamental laws of physics, the most basic of which would emerge as invariant with respect to those metaphysical possibilities.

The overall story that must be narrated here runs as follows: Nature—physical reality as we have it—represents the actualization of certain possibilities. But underlying this existential condition of affairs is the operation of a prior sub- or metaphysical principle, operative within the wider domain of logical possibility, and dividing this domain into disjoint sectors of 'real' and 'purely theoretical' possibility. To put it very figuratively, logical possibilities are involved in a virtual struggle for existence in which the axiologically best win out so as to become real possibilities. Specifically, when there are (mutually exclusive) alternatives that are possible in theory, nevertheless none will be a real or ontological possibility for realization as actual or as true if some other alternative is superior to it. The availability of a better alternative disqualifies its inferiors from qualifying as ontologically available—as *real*, that is, metaphysical—possibilities. And so whenever there is a uniquely best alternative, then this alternative is *ipso facto* realized as actual or true.

Optimalism is certainly a teleological theory: it holds that nature's *modus operandi* manifests a tropism towards a certain end or *telos*, to wit, optimization. The upshot represents a doctrine of final causes in Aristotle's sense. But this axiology is emphatically not a causal theory in the nowadays standard sense of efficient causation. It does not— and does not need to—regard value as a somehow efficient cause, a productive agency. On the contrary—value is not productive at all, but merely eliminative in so functioning as to block the way to availability of inferior productions. It does not drive causal processes but only canalizes or delimits them by ruling certain theoretical (or logical) possibilities out of the realm of real possibility. Consider an analogy. The English language allows double letters in its words, but not triple letters. But that does not mean that the double s of 'pussy' *causes* that ss-successive letter to be something different from s. It merely imposes a structural constraint of possibility. The lawful principle at issue explains the factual situation without any invocation of causality, seeing that an explanation via inherent constraints on possibility is not a causal explanation at all.

At this point a sceptical reader will doubtless ask, 'Given a spectrum of possibility with a tripartite structure such as (1) (2) (3), what would be the difference between an elimination that excludes the *A* of actuality from compartment 3 and thereby impels it to the two leftmost compartments numbered 1 and 2, and a magnetic-style attraction that that *causes A* to move towards the left and thereby out of compartment 3? Is the effect not the same either way?'

And this point is well taken—as far as it goes. But it overlooks something important.

The fact is that an attractive force requires a causal agency of some sort. On the other hand, possibility exclusions—the sheer unavailability of alternatives—can simply root in the general *modus operandi* of things without any reference to causal agency. Consider an analogy. Suppose that a society exhibits a suicide rate of 1.2 per 1,000 per annum during a certain era of its existence. No positive force is at work in constraining it to meet its quota of suicides—no identifiable cause engenders this aggregate result. And while it is effectively impossible to have a suicideless year, this lies in the nature of things generally and not in the potency of some suicide-impelling power or force. Again, more than 5 per cent of the letters on the first page of tomorrow's *Times* newspaper will be Es. But no force or power compels this effect. And while it is literally impossible for no Es to occur there and the nature of the situation precludes this prospect, there is no force of attraction to constrain the presence of Es. It is inevitable that there be more Es than Zs but this result is not the product of any power or force. This result is not produced by some *ad hoc* energy or agency—it is simply a feature of how things work in this context.

In explaining why physical objects and events exist we must indeed invoke causes and effects. But laws of nature themselves do not 'exist' as causal products—they just *obtain*. Now when laws obtain, there is, no doubt, a reason for their obtaining (an axiological reason, as we ourselves see it). But this reason can presumably be provided by an explanatory principle that need not carry us into the order of *efficient* causality through the motivations of an agent. To insist upon asking how values are able to function causally in law-realization is simply to adopt an inappropriate model for the processes involved. Value-explanation just is not causal: values do not function in the order of efficient causality at all. The Law of Optimality yields those results not via the mysterious attractive power of optimal possibilities but because suboptimal possibilities are excluded because their superior rivals simply pre-empt their place in possibility space. Axiogenetic theory has it that even as the presence of light displaces darkness so does the availability of better alternatives preclude the very possibility of those inferior so-called alternatives. The intervention of a productive agent or agency is not required.

And so in essence this line of reply concedes that value does not engender existence in the mode of efficient causations and that it would indeed be rather mysterious if values were asked to play a *causal* role in regard to laws. But this is to be seen as irrelevant. The real point is that while value does not efficiently *cause* existence it nevertheless *explains* it, exactly because causal explanation is not the only sort of explanation there is. And so the fact that axiology does not provide such an explanation is not an occasion for appropriate complaint. It does not stop value explanations from being explanations. They present perfectly good answers to 'Why is something-or-other so?' questions. It is just that in relation to laws, values play only an explanatory role through possibility elimination and not a causally productive role through actual creation. And this is no defect because a productive process is simply not called for.

And so, while axiological explanations fail to address a question for which design explanations have an answer—namely the causal question, 'How do values operate productively so as to bring particular laws to actualization?'—this reflects no demerit. For this question is simply inappropriate in the axiological setting. Values don't 'operate' in the causal order at all. They function only—and quite inefficiently—as constraints within the manifold of possibility. The issue of a specifically causal efficacy simply does not arise with axiological explanation.

What we have here, then, is not the operation of some rather mysterious force or agency but the preclusion (or rarefaction) of certain (theoretical) possibilities owing to the operation of natural law: a combination of the space of possibility from a wider range of hypothetical possibility to a narrow range of mimic possibility under the aegis of lawful principles—and optimality principle in the present case. (Here 'direct' pre-empts the prospect of a deeper explanation in terms of further principles relating to the operation of the powers or forces of some agent or agency.) The point is that the regress of explanatory principles must have a stop and that it is here—with axiology—that we reach a natural terminus by way of self-explanation. The long and short of it is that axio-ontology can be autonomous and nomically self-sufficient: it does not need to be seen as based in the operative power of some productive force or power or agency.

From the angle of explanation, a final causality of value thus has substantial advantages over a final causality of purpose. To be sure, both represent modes of final rather than efficient causation, since in both cases we deal with tendencies towards the realization of some prespecifiable condition of things. But these two forms of teleology are altogether distinct. The former explains regularities in terms of their conduciveness to some purposive agent's aims and objectives ('he never mixes business with pleasure'). The latter explains them through an in-principle universal force that exerts an operative value-impetus such as efficiency or economy. Accordingly, the axiological explanation of laws is a matter of nomological constraint based on values, and not a matter of efficient causality at all. In this regard it is a causality in name only.

If such an axiogenetic explanation is to work, then since there is only one real world the manifold of real possibilities must ultimately be reduced to one. That is, a series of successively operable value considerations must reduce the manifold of theoretical possibilities more and more restrictively until at last, as with the little Indians of the story, there remains but a single one. And that one is, in a very real sense, necessitated: it is, so to speak, constrained by value.

Does this necessitation bespeak a Spinozistic determinism? Will it engender a 'block universe' whose every detail is deterministically necessitated? By no means. The necessitation at issue relates to the *why* of the universe and not to its *what*. It is not only conceivable but presumably actual that the best possible world whose existence is axiologically necessitated by value considerations is one which in its internal mode of functioning provides for the contingencies of chance and free agency. The necessitation at issue here must emphatically *not* be construed as a matter of occurrence-necessitation as this is standardly construed in metaphysical deliberations about causal determinism.

8.5. The Value Efficacy Objection and the Theological Aspect

But what of the theological dimension?

Optimalism must come to terms with the complaint: 'Values are inherently anthropomorphic: only through constituting the motives of agents can values possibly obtain explanatory efficacy. Only by serving as some deliberate agent's motivational repertoire can a value come into effective operation.' And this line of thought leads to the objection:

> The axiological explanation of nature's laws with reference to values is not really self-sufficient. Without recourse to the productive agency of a creator God, the question of how values secure their functional efficacy remains unresolved. For how can values in and of themselves ever acquire their *modus operandi* in the determination of laws? Only design explanations can offer us an answer here: values are brought to bear on the world through the divine will which governs the productive agency of God.

This line of thought demands an answer to the question of how values can possibly figure in the realization of things save through the mediation of the purposes of a creatively active being—a finite agent with mundane things and with the universe as a whole, who else but God. We may characterize this as a theistically based value-efficacy objection. It clearly poses a challenge with which an axiological theory of explanation must come to terms.

Such a view of value-explanation is nothing new: it has existed in embryo since Plato's day thanks to his conception of demiurge. The basic idea is that the only way in which values can be brought to bear in the explanation of phenomena is through the mediation of a creative agent. Accordingly, thinkers from classical antiquity onwards have defended (or attacked) the principle that explaining the presence of order in nature—the fact that the world is a cosmos—requires postulating a creative intelligence as its cause. That nature manifests and exemplifies such cognitive values as order, harmony, uniformity was thus explained by regarding these as marks of purpose. On this basis, the mainstream of Western thought regarding axiological explanation has taken the line that there is a supernatural agent (God, demiurge, cosmic spirit) and that values obtain their explanatory bearing by influencing the state of mind which governs his creative endeavours. This essentially *purposive* approach characterizes the traditional argument from design, which explains the creation with reference to a creator (as its *ratio essendi*) and infers the existence of this creator from the orderly structure of created nature (as his *ratio cognoscendi*).[17] The sequential explanatory slide from design to value to purpose to intelligence was historically seen as inexorable. And so the idea of a recourse to an explanatory principle that is geared to values without any such mediation represents a radical departure. The guiding conception of the present deliberations—that value is the natural place to sever this chain—reflects a break with a longstanding tradition.

However, the justification of this break lies in observing the important distinction between values and purposes. Granted, a purpose must be *somebody's* purpose: it must have some intelligent agent as its owner-operator. It lies in the very nature of the concept that purposes cannot exist in splendid isolation; they must, in the final analysis, belong to some agent or other. For purposes as such, to be is to be adopted. Purposive explanations operate in terms of why conscious agent do things, and not ones of why impersonal conditions obtain.

A value, however, can be altogether impersonal. Being a value does not require that somebody actually values it (any more than being a fact requires that somebody actually realizes it). A person can certainly hold a certain value dear but if it indeed is a value, then its status as such is no more dependent on its actually being valued than the symmetry of a landscape depends on its actually being discerned. Values admit of being prized, but that does not mean that they actually are, any more than a task's being difficult means that anyone actually attempts it. To be of value is to *deserve* to be valued, but that of course need not actually happen: the value of things can be underestimated or overestimated or totally overlooked. Neither the items that have value not the facts of their being of value depend on

---

[17] For a useful collection of relevant texts see Donald R. Burrill, *The Cosmological Argument: A Spectrum of Opinion* (Garden City, NY: Anchor Books, 1967). Two interesting recent accounts of the issues and their historical ramifications include: Rowe, *The Cosmological Argument*; and Craig, *The Cosmological Argument From Plato to Leibniz*.

apprehending minds for their reality. And this holds in particular for ontological values such as economy, simplicity, regularity, uniformity, etc., that figure in the axiological explanation of laws. The being of values does *not* consist in their being perceived, any more than does the being of most other sorts of things.

When someone *adopts* a certain value, then fostering or promoting it can of course become one of his purposes. 'Promoting friendship among the members' can function exactly as 'getting elected president of the club' in regard to being someone's purpose. But values as such ('simplicity', for example) are not purposes any more than offices ('being president') are—though, of course, their promotion or more ample realization may well function as somebody's purpose. The crucial point is that the *being* of a value does not consist in its being adopted by someone, any more than the being of a truth consists in its being endorsed by someone.

Just here is where the shift from purpose to value explanation is decisively advantageous. A purpose must be somebody's purpose, and if something has a purpose at all then it must be that it serves *somebody's* purposes. But in this regard purpose differs from value where less baggage is required. While people indeed can value things, something can be of value—can *have* value—without being valued *by* anybody—not even God. (It must be valuable *for* something or other but it need not be valued *by* somebody; in principle clean air can be valuable for mammals without being valued *by* any of them.)

In general, then, we need not embed values in purposes; axiological explanation can stand on its own feet. Axiological existence-explanation can thus proceed entirely outside the purposive order. In taking the axiological route, one is not saying that the realization of value is reality's purpose. We need not personify nature to account for its features. To say that nature embodies value is a very far cry from saying that the realization of value is one of its purposes. That reality operates in a certain manner—that its *modus operandi* follows certain laws or principles—is in general an entirely impersonal thesis. The values involved in axiological explanation need not be *somebody's* values. No element of personification, no reference to anyone's aims or purposes, need be involved in axiological explanation. Purpose, on the other hand, necessarily requires a purposer—it must be *somebody's* purpose. In this regard, value stands with order rather than with purpose. Order-seeking in nature does not presuppose an orderer, nor value-seeking a valuer. The maintenance of enhancement of a value can be a matter of blind operation of impersonal forces or factors.

In this respect, the present axiological approach differs decisively from that of Leibniz. He answered the question, 'Why is it that the value-optimizing world should be the one that actually exists?' with reference to the will of a God who *chooses* to adopt value optimization as a creative principle. Leibniz was committed to an idea that it is necessary to account for the obtaining of a principle in terms of the operation of an existing entity (specifically the agency of an intelligent being—namely God). Instead, our axiological approach sees the explanatory bearing of a principle of value as direct, without mediation through the agency of a substantial being (however extraordinary) as final and fundamental.[18] On grounds of explanatory economy, at least, purpose is thus something that we would be well advised to manage without if we can actually manage to do so.

Altogether different explanatory processes are thus at issue in axiological and in purposive explanation, and the ontological requirements of the former are a great deal more modest than those of the latter. To hold that nature operates so as to minimize or maximize this or that evaluative factor does *not* commit us to presupposing a purposive agency at work in or behind nature. The rationale of value can be self-contained; it can stay clear of any involvement with matters of causality, agency, and purpose. Values, in sum, can affect the constitution of reality directly through serving as possibility constraints rather than mediately through the aims and objectives of agents.

8.6. Value Naturalism

Given that it is values rather than purposes that function in axiological explanation, these explanations can be entirely impersonal. Values here function directly rather than via the mediation of agents.

---

[18] Our metaphysical invocation of a principle of value is akin to A. C. Ewing's theological application of similar ideas in his interesting article 'Two "Proofs" of God's Existence', *Religious Studies*, 1 (1961), 29–45. Ewing there propounds the argument that God's existence is to be accounted for axiologically: that he exists 'because it was supremely good that God should exist' (p. 35). This approach has the substantial merit of avoiding Leibniz's tactic of grounding the efficacy of value in a pre-existing deity by contemplating the prospect that value is so fundamental that the deity itself can be accounted for in its terms.

The idea is simply that the system in question is value-tropic (as it were) in that it inherently tends to realize certain value-endowed conditions (maintaining stability, achieving symmetry, prolonging longevity, operating efficiently, etc.). But, of course, the system that comports itself in this way need not overtly hold such a value—like a physical system that pursues the path of least resistance, it may well be the sort of thing for which the conscious adoption of values is simply not possible. To re-emphasize: when its *modus operandi* establishes commitment to a certain value, nature need not seek value any more than water need seek its own level. We need not anthropomorphize here, even as a claim to end-directed transactions in the world ('Nature abhors a vacuum') is without any implications about a purposively operating mind. A system can be goal-directed through its inherent natural programming (e.g. heliotropism or homeostasis) without any admixture of purpose even as a conservation of energy principle need not be held on the basis of nature's seeking to conserve energy. For there is no good reason why an axiology cannot or should not take the form of a value naturalism. On the contrary. To implement the principle of axiology by way of *personification* would be self-defeating, since we ideally want to explain existence in a way that is self-sustaining (self-contained, ultimate).

To be sure, *why* nature so operates as to implement the value *V* will require some explanation. But as we have seen the prospect of self-invoking explanations is available here. For example: nature fosters economy (simplicity, harmony, etc.) because that is the most economical of things for it to do. Or again: why do its laws exist as they do? Because that's for the axiological best in optimizing the systemic operations that obtain. And why does what is for the best obtain— just exactly because that itself is for the best. The explanation of the operation of laws is axiological (value-referential). And the explanation of the obtaining of values is self-referential—i.e. is also axiological. The possibility of providing an explanation on its own basis—a reflexive explanation that is literally a self-explanation—is now before us. Value is, or can be, regress-stopping: it can be 'final' by way of being self-explanatory in a manner purpose cannot be.

The axiology at issue should thus be seen as naturalistic. The values involved are to encompass factors like stability, symmetry, continuity, complexity, order, and even a dynamic impetus to the development of 'higher' forms possessed of more sophisticated capabilities—perhaps even a sort of Hegelian impetus towards the evolutionary emergence of a creature possessed of an intelligence able to comprehend and appreciate the universe itself, creating a conscious reduplication model of the universe in the realm of thought through the artifice of intelligence. So in any event these values are mundane and non-transcendental, pivoting on physico-metaphysical factors that make for an altogether 'naturalistic' axiology that can be posited on the basis of the world's observable features.[19] After all, it is plausible to take the naturalistic line that in reasoning from the character of nature we should remain in the natural realm. Whatever values we may find to inhere in the operations of nature are still something natural—there need be nothing supranatural (let alone supernatural!) about it. A universe that functions under the aegis of value no more requires an underlying extra-natural valuer than a universe that exhibits lawful order necessarily requires an extra-natural lawgiver or a universe that has a start in time (the 'Big Bang') necessarily requires an extra-natural creator. The values at issue can, in principle, function wholly within the *modus operandi* of nature. Value-tropism requires the support of a natural-external intelligence no more than a principle of conservation or a principle of least action does.

But are those naturalistic metaphysical 'values' not really problematic as such owing to their cold-blooded indifference to matters of human welfare and well-being? Not necessarily. For surely a world whose ontological make-up permits and perhaps even facilitates the emergence of intelligent creatures is thereby automatically such that those ontological entities are likely to carry genuinely human values in their train. Thus, for example, as C. S. Peirce insisted, a universe that permits the emergence of intelligent beings must itself be in some degree intelligible.

8.7. Sidestepping Theology

And so, confronted with the challenge, 'What if one is sceptical about theism? Would one then not have to reject optimalism?' The optim-

---

[19] It might seem at first thought that a reality that emerges under the aegis of physico-metaphysical values is cold-bloodedly indifferent to the welfare of intelligent beings. But this is in fact unlikely. For such an existential manifold is by its very nature a (quasi-rational) order that is bound to be congenial to the creatures—and especially the *intelligent* creatures—that evolve within it. (What we have here is a position that is a hybrid crossing of Leibniz and Darwin.)

alist replies: 'Not at all. Optimalism does not presuppose theism—it perhaps could but certainly need not call upon God to institute optimalism.'

To reach outside the value domain itself to equip value with a purposive explanation that is theological in nature is unnecessary and counterproductive—it complicates rather than simplifies the explanatory process. For we then cannot avoid the question: 'Why does the putative creator adopt this purpose?' The response must take the form that he deems (and of course, since it is God that is at issue, *rightly* deems) it to be of value. And this at once carries us back to axiology. Recourse to divine purpose merely adds a complex epicycle once the question of the rational validity of this purpose arises. We now have a two-factor explanation of creator plus value, where in principle a one-factor explanation in terms of value as such can accomplish the explanatory task.

Following the guidelines of Kant's *Critique of Teleological Judgment*, Archbishop Temple wrote: 'The chain of causes is not self-explanatory... There is in fact only one principle which is self-explanatory; it is Purpose. When in tracing any causal nexus we read the activity of a will fulfilling a Purpose with which we ourselves sympathize, we are in fact satisfied.'[20] But this is very problematic because purpose clearly does not stand at the end of the explanatory line. A rational agent's purposes always have a rationale: the *that* of purpose leaves open the question, *why*? It is altogether appropriate to inquire why an agent *A* adopts a particular purpose *P*: the question of the rationale for that purpose cannot be avoided. The good archbishop is simply wrong to think of purpose as an explanatory ultimate. However much we may sympathize with someone's purposes, they will still remain items on the explanatory agenda. If you are famished, then however thoroughly I may understand your plight, your purpose of getting food still needs (and is capable of receiving) an explanation—in terms of hunger satisfaction immediately, and ultimately in terms of the value of pain avoidance. The operation of a rationally adopted purpose must itself always root in a value of some sort: well-being in the present case. The explanation is doubtless eminently simple and straightforward, but its being obvious is something quite different from its being superfluous.

[20] *Contemporary British Philosophy, First Series*, ed. J. H. Muirhead (London: Allen Unwin, 1925), 418.

The salient difference between the present axiological approach and the traditional theological argumentation from design thus turns on keeping values apart from divine intentions and purposes. To say that reality is subject to an evaluative principle is emphatically not to personify nature or to personalize the productive forces that serve to explain it. There is enormous confusion in the philosophical tradition on this point. Early on, Anaximander of Miletus and other Presocratic nature philosophers were prepared to do without the idea that cosmic order requires an orderer. But Plato, and especially Christian Neoplatonism, entrenched this idea in Western philosophy almost beyond recall. And yet this stance is eminently questionable. For one simply need not locate the source of value in a personal creator, a divine mind or spirit that is an agent whose creative actions are animated by a desire for the good. Hume, Kant, and the numberless post-Darwinian anti-teleologists to the contrary notwithstanding, the conception that order requires an orderer still continues to be deeply entrenched. And yet this temptation must be resisted—order no more requires an orderer or value a valuer than temperature demands a heat-sensitively sentient being. Value itself is taken to constitute a determinative force, capable on its own footing of providing a principle of explication without the mediation of a personal agent for whom it serves as a determining motive.

In the nineteenth century, William Whewell wrote, 'The examination of the material world brings before us a number of things and relations of things which suggest to most minds the beliefs of a creating and presiding Intelligence.'[21] And many theorists from Leibniz to Einstein have held exactly this same view.[22] But the history of science—where God has been asked to do less and less explanatory work over the course of time—is such as to make it reasonable to contemplate an account of design without recourse to a designer. Our axiogenetic theory is thus without theological demands or implications. And this is all to the good. For David Hume's point holds good: that nature is the product of the operations of a designing intelligence is not something we can learn convincingly merely from a study of the workings of nature itself.

---

[21] William Whewell, *Astronomy and General Physics Considered with Reference to Natural Theology* (London: H. G. Bohn, 1852), 1.

[22] See Lewis S. Feuer, 'Noumenalism and Einstein's Argument for the Existence of God', *Inquiry*, 26 (1981), 251–85.

Accordingly, axiology need not be tied to religion as this enterprise is usually understood.[23] It may be tempting for us anthropomorphizing humans to ground nature's elegant laws in the mathematicized planning of an Originative Intelligence, but the merit of an axiological approach shows that this temptation can—and should—be resisted. From the days of Laplace and Darwin onwards, it has become increasingly clear that design *in* nature does not entail a designer *of* nature, a purposing intelligence 'behind' nature, a creator God. The axiological explanation of nature and its laws circumvents the cosmological argument rather than engendering some version of it.

To be sure, axiological explanation is not *incompatible* with theism—on the contrary, it is thoroughly congenial to it. (A benign Creator would certainly create a duly optimal world.) But a theory of axiological ontogenesis certainly does not *require* a further recourse to the theological domain. What is at issue here is not an *odium theologicum*—an aversion to theological considerations as such. It is rather the idea of the medieval dictum *non in philosophia recurrere est ad deum*—that we should not ask God to pull our philosophical chestnuts out of the fire.[24] God has more important work to do than helping philosophers out of the corners into which they paint themselves. This said, however, it must be stressed that axiological explanation is altogether congenial to theism—even though they do not require it. After all it is only to be expected that if the world is created by a God of a sort that the tradition encourages us to accept, then the world that such a God creates should be one in which values play a role. And so it would seem that theism requires axiological explanation distinctly more than axiological explanation requires theism.

Questions like, 'Why is there anything at all?' are at bottom naturalistic questions and they ought ideally to be answered by

---

[23] To be sure, some idealists envision a religion in which God plays so small a role that even the present theory can count as 'religious'. J. M. E. McTaggart, for example, defined religion as 'an emotion resting on a connection of a harmony between ourselves and the universe at large'. (*Some Dogmas of Religion* (London: E. Arnold, 1906), 3). But, of course, since we humans are ourselves an evolved part of nature, some degree of affective harmony is pretty well inevitable in a way that need not have much of 'religion' about it on any ordinary understanding of the matter.

[24] Indeed an over-enthusiastic optimalist could take the line that theism hinges on optimalism rather than the reverse, arguing that God's own existence issues from optimalism: he exists because that's for the best.

naturalistic means. After all, to explain the natural realm in super-natural terms is surely an epistemically problematic proceeding. It is a matter of explaining something we understand rather imperfectly in terms of something we really do not understand at all (namely God). As an integral part of natural reality we ourselves have at least some cognitive grip upon it. But the ways of God are so far and above our comprehension that here indeed we do confront an authentic mystery. To explain nature's features in supernatural terms involves explaining *obscurum per obscurior*.

But axiogenesis must surely be rejected because it is so strange, even weird. Really? Is it any stranger than much that we encounter in science—for example, the current theories of the physics of the very small or the very large? Clearly when you ask extraordinary questions you must be prepared for extraordinary answers. That the theories that do the job in any domain of issues extremely remote from the realm of everyday experience should seem weird by everyday standards is only natural and to be expected. Weirdness, by the standards of everyday familiarity, is no cogent objection here—it is something that we have to expect. Yet is such a theory of axiological ontogenesis not defeated by the objection: If it really were the case that value explains existence, then why isn't the world altogether perfect?

The answer lies in the inherent complexity of value. An object that is of any value at all is subject to a *complex* of values. For it is the fundamental fact of axiology that every evaluation-admitting object has a *plurality* of evaluative features. Take a car—an automobile. Here the relevant parameters of merit clearly include such factors as speed, reliability, repair infrequency, safety, operating economy, aesthetic appearance, road-handling ability. But in actual practice such features are interrelated. It is unavoidable that they trade off against one another: more of A means less of B. It would be ridiculous to have a supersafe car with a maximum speed of 2 miles per hour. It would be ridiculous to have a car that is inexpensive to operate but spends three-quarters of the time in a repair shop. It is an inherently inevitable feature of the nature of things—an inevitable 'fact of life'—that value realization is always a matter of balance, of trade-offs, of compromise. The reality of it is that value factors always compete in matters of realization. A concurrent maximum in *every* dimension is simply unavoidable in this (or indeed any other realis-tically conceivable) world. All that one can ever reasonably ask for is an auspicious combination of values. Perfection—maximum realization of every value dimension all at once—is simply unrealizable because of the interaction of parameters: in designing a car you cannot maximize both safety and economy of operation. Analogously the world is not absolutely perfect—perfect in *every* respect—because this sort of absolute perfection is in principle impossible of realization. And of course it makes no sense to ask for the impossible. Accordingly, the objection, 'If value is the key to existence, the world would be perfect', collapses. All that will follow on axiogenetic principles is that the world will exemplify an optimal interactive balance of the relevant natural factors. An optimally realizable best need not be perfect in the naïve sense of that term which unrealistically demands maximality in every relevant respect.

Leibniz had the right approach here: optimalism does not maintain that the world is absolutely perfect but just that it be the best that is possible—that it outranks the available alternatives.

What the optimalist can and should do is to insist that because of the intricate inherent interrelationships among value parameters an imperfection in this or that respect must be taken in one's stride because they have to be there for an optimal overall combination of value to be realized. What prevents optimalism from being too Pollyanna-ish to be plausible is the deeply pessimistic acknowledgement that even the best of possible arrangements is bound to exhibit very real shortcomings. It is an inherently inevitable feature of the nature of things—an inevitable fact of life—that value realization is always a matter of balance, of trade-offs, of compromise. The reality of it is that value factors always compete in matters of realization. A concurrent maximum in *every* dimension is simply unavoidable in this (or indeed any other realistically conceivable) world. All that one can ever reasonably ask for is an auspicious combination of values.

And so the objection, 'If value is the key to existence, the world would be perfect', proves to be untenable. All that will follow on axiogenetic principles is that the world will exemplify an optimal balance of the relevant evaluative factors.

But what of the epistemic dimension. What sort of *evidence* speaks for axiogenesis? What sorts of grounds are there for claiming that what is for the best actually exists?

Of course, with matters of synoptic explanation we are dealing with issues that go above and beyond the resources of observation.

The rationale of reality-as-a-whole is clearly not going to be something that is directly observable—it will have to be a theoretical entity—or, rather, a theoretical fact. Like all other such facts it will have links to observation, but they will almost certainly be very long-distance links that provide for only a rather loose coupling. The validation at issue here certainly cannot dispense with matters of observation but it will inevitably have to go far above and beyond them—much as in other branches of theoretical science. It is unavoidable that the explanatory requisites of this problem-domain should be not supernatural, to be sure, but in some respects supranatural. For it is, after all, the explanation of nature's nature that is at issue.

In general we verify abstract theses by monitoring the acceptability of their concrete consequences. And there is no reason not to apply this general principle in the present case as well. Of course it all depends; specifically it depends on the standard of merit or value that we employ. Clearly if the standard is one of such specifically human-advantage value as comfort, peace of mind, security of existence, or the like, then this claim becomes very problematic and questionable. But if the values at issue are less blatantly anthropomorphic and more metaphysical—if they look to such factors as nomic order under the aegis of natural laws congenial to the progressive development of life and intelligence—then matters appear in a less problematic light. Axiogenesis has to be seen as a confirmable thesis whose evidentiation hinges on the systematizing of our knowledge of nature's ways. The crux would now be a framework of natural law engendering a course of progressive development whose successive phases of cosmic, biological, and rational evolution provide for the emergence of intelligent life-forms able not only to understand nature under the aegis of science but also to appreciate it under the aegis of religion. What is pivotal here is thus not just a lawful order in nature but a lawful order able to provide an effective pathway alike to a scientific understanding and an affective appreciation of the real. But these are matters that have to emerge from inquiry. Philosophical deliberations can do no more than show that the doctrine is available as a plausible theoretical prospect that enjoys certain theoretical advantages over its alternatives. But its acceptability will ultimately have to hinge on the progress of science itself.

APPENDIX

As already noted, the axio-ontological position set out here is clearly indebted to the teachings of G. W. Leibniz. More recently, a kindred position has been defended by the Canadian philosopher John Leslie.[25] There are, however, substantial differences between Leslie's approach and that of the present discussion.

Leslie's position is predicated on a recourse to specifically *ethical* considerations so that for him 'the world's existence and make-up' are products of 'a directly active ethical necessity' with the result that 'ethical requirements are creatively powerful'.[26]

On this basis, Leslie contemplates a productive agent or agency which, while not necessarily identifiable with God, is nevertheless a being whose creative action is thereby appraisable in the category of right/wrong. As Leslie sees it, ethically guided dutiful agency is the crux, and reality is the creation of a power or agency that functions subject to the impulse of ethical considerations. And he has little alternative to such a producer-anthropomorphism since ethical considerations are by nature agent-co-ordinated, having to function as link between producer and product. By their very nature, ethical factors are causally productive only by way of motivation.

No such anthropomorphism invades the present axiological account. It sees the real as emerging from the manifold of possibility in a way that is altogether natural. That is to say it sees this manifold as subject to inherently value-oriented principles of operation that serve to condense a plurality of possibilities down to a unique alternative, so that among a multitude of logical possibilities only a single real possibility remains, which is actualized in virtue of this very fact. The world thus exists of necessity all right, but the necessity in question is not logical but metaphysical or axiological in nature. The aspect of productive agency that is crucial to Leslie's *deontological* ontogenesis—as it was to that of Leibniz—is altogether absent from the present *axiological* ontogenesis.

---

[25] He initially expounded it in a paper entitled 'The Theory that the World Exists Because it Should', *American Philosophical Quarterly*, 7 (1970), 286–98, and subsequently developed it more fully in his book *Value and Existence* (Oxford: Clarendon Press, 1979). See also his paper 'The World's Necessary Existence', *International Journal for Philosophy of Religion*, 18 (1980), 207–23 and his book *Universes* (New York: Routledge, 1996).

[26] John Leslie, 'The Theory that the World Exists Because It Should', 268.

And so, in the end, the present axiological approach differs decisively from that of Leibniz and his latter-day congeners such as John
Leslie. They propose to answer the question, 'Why is it that the value-
optimizing world should be the one that actually exists?' with reference to the will of a God who *chooses* to adopt value optimization as a
creative principle. Leibniz—as we saw at the outset—was committed
to an idea that it is necessary to account for the obtaining of a
principle in terms of the operation of an existing entity (specifically
the agency of an intelligent being—namely God). Instead, an axiological approach sees the explanatory bearing of a principle of value
as direct, without mediation through the agency of a substantial
being (however extraordinary) as final and fundamental.[27] On
grounds of explanatory economy, at least, purpose is thus something
that we would be well advised to forgo if we can actually manage to
do so.

The key factor here is not ethical motivation but ontological
constraint. For the values contemplated in the present discussion
are *ontological* rather than *ethical* values—that is, values within the
spectrum of good/bad rather than that of right/wrong.[28] Accordingly,
the present position prescinds from the requirement of a productive-
creative-active agency or power, instead viewing the effect of value
not in terms of productive exigency but rather in terms of exclusion.
Its operative principle is not the magnetic attraction that a consideration of the good exerts upon a creative agent but the eliminative
impetus within in the range of 'real' possibilities.

Leslie's axiological ontology pivots on the idea that ethics somehow requires existence. The present theory moves in the reverse
direction to stipulate that existence does (and axiologically must)
have a nature that paves the way to ethics: to the evolutionary
emergence of a creature capable of recognizing its duties in relation
to the furtherance of the good. Thus as in Big Bang cosmology, the
universe of cosmic evolution begins with physics and gives rise to
biology—let alone anthropology and psychology and ethics—only

---

[27] Our metaphysical invocation of a principle of value is akin to A. C. Ewing's theological application of similar ideas in his interesting article, 'Two "Proofs" of God's Existence',
Religious Studies, 1 (1961), 29–45. Ewing there propunds the argument that God's existence
is to be accounted for axiologically: that he exists 'because it was supremely good that God
should exist' (p. 35). This approach has the substantial merit of avoiding Leibniz's tactic of
grounding the efficacy of value in a pre-existing deity by contemplating the prospect that
value is so fundamental that the Deity itself can be accounted for in its terms.
[28] Recall the Moore–Sidgwick controversy discussed in 8.2 above.

late in the game. As axiogenesis sees it, *ontological* values are primary and basic, while specifically *ethical* values emerge on the world stage only in eventual due course with the evolutionary emergence of intelligent agents.

Bibliography

ALMEDER, ROBERT, *Blind Realism* (Lanham, Md.: Rowman & Littlefield, 1992).

AMALDI, EDOARDO, 'The Unity of Physics', *Physics Today*, 261 (Sept. 1973), 23–9.

BACON, FRANCIS, *Novum organum*.

BARROW, JOHN D., and TIPLER FRANK T., *The Anthropic Cosmological Principle* (Oxford: Clarendon Press, 1986).

BARTLETT, S. J., and SUBER, P. (eds.), *Self-Reference* (Dordrecht: Marttinus Nijhoff, 1987).

BRANDON, ROBERT N., *Adaptation and Environment* (Princeton: Princeton University Press, 1990).

BREUER, THOMAS, 'Universal and unvollständig: Theorien über alles?', *Philosophia Naturalis*, 34 (1997), 1–20.

BUNGE, MARIO, *The Myth of Simplicity* (Englewood Cliffs, NJ: Prentice Hall, 1963).

—— *Scientific Research* (2 vols.; New York: Springer, 1967).

BURRILL, DONALD R., *The Cosmological Argument: A Spectrum of Opinion* (Garden City, NY: Anchor Books, 1967).

CARTWRIGHT, NANCY, *How the Laws of Physics Lie* (Oxford: Clarendon Press, 1983).

CHAMPLAIN, T. S., *Reflexive Paradoxes* (London: Routledge, 1988).

CHURCHLAND, PATRICIA, *Neurophilosophy: Towards a Unified Theory of the Mind-Brain* (Cambridge, Mass.: MIT Press, 1986).

CHURCHLAND, PAUL, 'Eliminative Materialism and Propositional Attitudes', *The Journal of Philosophy*, 78 (1983).

CRAIG, WILLIAM LANE, *The Cosmological Argument from Plato to Leibniz* (London: Macmillan, 1980).

DAVIDSON, DONALD, 'The Very Idea of a Conceptual Scheme', *Proceedings and Addresses of the American Philosophical Association*, 47 (1973–4), 5–20.

DAWKIN, RICHARD, *The Blind Watchmaker* (New York: Norton, 1986).

DRACHMANN, A. G., *The Mechanical Technology of Greek and Roman Antiquity* (Madison: University of Wisconsin Press, 1963).

DUMMETT, MICHAEL, 'Truth', *Proceedings of the Aristotelian Society*, 59 (1958–9).

DUPRÉ, JOHN, *The Disorder of Things: Metaphysical Foundations of the Disunity of Science* (Cambridge, Mass.: Harvard University Press, 1993).

EDDINGTON, A. S., *The Nature of the Physical World* (Cambridge: Cambridge University Press, 1928).

EHRENSVÄRD, GÖSTA, *Man on Another World* (Chicago: University of Chicago Press, 1965).

EINSTEIN, ALBERT, *Lettres à Maurice Solovine* (New York: Philosophical Library, 1987).

EWING, A. C., 'Two "Proofs" of God's Existence', *Religious Studies*, 1 (1961), 29–45.

FECHER, VINCENT JULIAN, *Error, Deception, and Incomplete Truth* (Rome: Officium Libri Catholici, 1975).

FEUER, LEWIS S., 'Noumenalism and Einstein's Argument for the Existence of God', *Inquiry*, 26 (1981), 251–85.

GALE, RICHARD M., *On the Nature and Existence of God* (Cambridge: Cambridge University Press, 1991).

GALILEO, GALILEI, *Dialogo 2, Le Opere di Galileo Galilei*, Edizione Nationale, (20 vols.; Florence, 1890–1909).

GINZBERG, V. L., *Key Problems of Physics and Astrophysics*, tr. O. Glevov (Moscow: MIR Publishing House, 1978).

GRIM, PATRICK, *The Incomplete Universe: Totality, Knowledge, and Truth* (Cambridge, Mass.: MIT Press, 1991).

GUT, ALLAN, and STEINHARDT, P. J., 'Grand Unified Theories', *The Encyclopedia of Cosmology*, ed. N. S. Hetherington (New York: Garland Publishing, 1993).

HEMPEL, CARL G., 'Science Unlimited', *The Annals of the Japan Association for Philosophy of Science*, 14 (1973), 187–202.

HEMPEL, CARL G., and OPPENHEIM, PAUL, 'Studies in Logic of Explanation', *Philosophy of Science*, 15 (1948), 135–75.

HESSE, MARY, *Revolutions and Reconstructions in the Philosophy of Science* (Bloomington, Ind.: University of Indiana Press, 1980).

HOLLAND, JOHN H., *Hidden Order: How Adaptation Builds Complexity* (Reading, Mass.: Addison-Wesley, 1995).

HUME, DAVID, *Dialogues Concerning Natural Religion*, ed. N. K. Smith (London: Longmans Green, 1922).

JAMES, WILLIAM, *Pragmatism* (New York: Longmans Green, 1907).

KANT, IMMANUEL, *Critique of Pure Reason*.

KAUFMANN, STUART, *At Home in the Universe: The Search for the Laws of Self-Organization and Complexity* (New York: Oxford University Press, 1995).

KITCHER, PHILIP, 'Explanatory Unification', *Philosophy of Science*, 48 (1981), 507–31.

KUHN, THOMAS, *The Structure of Scientific Revolutions* (Chicago: University of Chicago Press, 1962).

LEIBNIZ, G. W. *Philosophische Schriften*, ed. C. I. Gerhardt (Berlin: Weidmann, 1890), vii.

—— *Philosophical Papers and Letters*, ed. L. E. Loemker, 2nd edn. (Dordrecht: D. Reidel, 1969).

LESLIE, JOHN, 'The Theory that the World Exists Because it Should', *American Philosophical Quarterly*, 7 (1970), 286–98.

—— *Value and Existence* (Oxford: Clarendon Press, 1979).

—— 'The World's Necessary Existence', *International Journal for Philosophy of Religion*, 18 (1980), 207–23.

—— *Universes* (New York: Routledge, 1996).

LEWIS, C. I., *An Analysis of Knowledge and Valuation* (La Salle, Ill.: Open Court, 1962).

MCTAGGART, J. M. E., *Some Dogmas of Religion* (London: E. Arnold, 1906).

MAIMONIDES, *The Guide for the Perplexed*, ed. M. Friedlauder (New York: Dover, 1956).

MAINZER, KLAUS, *Thinking in Complexity* (Berlin: Springer, 1997).

MOORE, G. E., *Principia Ethica* (Cambridge: University of Cambridge Press, 1903).

—— *Some Main Problems of Philosophy* (London: Allen & Unwin, 1953).

NAGEL, THOMAS, 'What is it Like to be a Bat?', *Mortal Questions* (Cambridge, Mass.: Harvard University Press, 1976).

NIINILUOTO, IIKKA, 'Scientific Progress', *Synthese*, 45 (1980).

PEIRCE, CHARLES SANDERS, *Collected Papers*, (7 vols.; Cambridge, Mass.: Harvard University Press, 1931–58).

PETLEY, B. W., *The Fundamental Physical Constants and the Frontiers of Measurement* (Bristol: Hilger, 1985).

PLATO, *Republic*.

POLKINGHORNE, J. C., *The Way the World Is* (Grand Rapids, Mich.: Eerdmans, 1984).

—— *One World: The Interaction of Science and Theology* (Princeton, NJ: Princeton University Press, 1986).

—— *Science and Creation: The Search for Understanding* (New York: Random House 1988).

—— *God's Action in the World* (Berkeley: Center of Theology and Natural Science Public Forums, 1990).

—— *The Faith of a Physicist: Reflections of a Bottom-up Thinker* (Princeton, NJ: Princeton University Press, 1994).

POPPER, K. R., *Realism and the Aim of Science* (London: Routledge, 1956).

—— *Logik der Forschung* (London: Hutchinson, 1959).

—— *Objective Knowledge: An Evolutionary Approach* (Oxford: Clarendon Press, 1972).

PRUSS, ALEXANDER R., 'The Hume–Edwards Principle and the Cosmological Argument', *International Journal for Philosophy of Religion*, 434 (1988), 149–65.

REDHEAD, MICHAEL, *From Physics to Metaphysics* (Cambridge: Cambridge University Press, 1995).

REICHENBACH, HANS, *Experience and Prediction* (Chicago: University of Chicago Press, 1938), 376.

RESCHER, NICHOLAS, *Conceptual Idealism* (Oxford: Blackwell, 1973).

—— *Scientific Progress* (Oxford: Basil Blackwell, 1976).

—— *Methodological Pragmatism* (Oxford: Basil Blackwell, 1977).

—— *Peirce's Philosophy of Science* (Notre Dame: University of Notre Dame Press, 1978).

—— *Cognitive Systematization* (Oxford: Basil Blackwell, 1979).

—— *Induction* (Oxford: Basil Blackwell, 1980).

—— *Empirical Inquiry* (Totowa, NJ: Rowman & Littlefield, 1982).

—— *The Limits of Science* (Berkeley: University of California Press, 1984).

—— *The Riddle of Existence* (Lanham, Md.: University Press of America, 1984).

—— *Scientific Realism* (Dordrecht: Kluwer Academic Publishers, 1987).

—— *Cognitive Economy* (Pittsburgh: University of Pittsburgh Press, 1989).

—— *A Useful Inheritance* (Savage, Md.: Rowman & Littlefield, 1990).

—— *Philosophical Standardism* (Pittsburgh: University of Pittsburgh Press, 1994).

—— 'H_2O: Hempel-Helmer-Oppenheim: An Episode in the History of Scientific Philosophy in the Twentieth Century', *Philosophy of Science*, 64 (1997), 779–805.

—— *Profitable Speculations* (Lanham, Md.: Rowman & Littlefield, 1997).

—— *Complexity* (New Brunswick, NJ: Transaction Publishers, 1998).

ROWE, WILLIAM L., *The Cosmological Argument* (Princeton: Princeton University Press, 1975).

SALMON, WESLEY, *Four Decades of Scientific Explanation* (Minneapolis: University of Minnesota Press, 1990).

SCHILPP, P. A. (ed.), *The Philosophy of Brand Blanshard* (La Salle, Ill.: Open Court, 1980).

SCHLICK, MORITZ, *Gesetz, Kausalität und Wahrscheinlichkeit* (Vienna: Gerold, 1948).

—— *Philosophy of Nature* (New York: Greenwood Press, 1968).

—— *Philosophical Papers* (Dordrecht: D. Reidel, 1979), i.

—— 'Positivism and Realism', *Synthese*, 7 (1932), 1–31.

SCHROEDINGER, ERWIN, *What is Life?* (Cambridge: Cambridge University Press, 1945).

SIDGWICK, HENRY, *Methods of Ethics* (London: Macmillan, 1874).

SIMMEL, GEORG, 'Über eine Beziehung der Selektionslehre zur Erkenntnistheorie', *Archiv für systematische Philosophie und Soziologie* (1895), i. 34–45.

SIMON, HERBERT A., *The Sciences of the Artificial* (Cambridge, Mass.: MIT Press, 1969).

SPENCER, HERBERT, *First Principles*, 7th edn. (London: Methuen, 1889).

STICH, STEPHEN, *From Folk Psychology to Cognitive Science: The Case Against Belief* (Cambridge, Mass.: MIT Press, 1983).

STRAWSON, P. F., 'Truth', *Proceedings of the Aristotelian Society*, suppl. vol. 24 (1950), 129–56.

TEMPLE, WILLIAM, *Contemporary British Philosophy, First Series*, ed. J. H. Muirhead (London: Allen & Unwin, 1925).

WEINBERG, STEVEN, *Dreams of a Final Theory* (New York: Pantheon, 1992).

WEIZSÄCKER, C. F. von, 'The Unity of Physics', in Ted Bastin (ed.) *Quantum Theory and Beyond* (Cambridge: Cambridge University Press, 1971).

WHEWELL, WILLIAM, *Astronomy and General Physics Considered with Reference to Natural Theology* (London: H. G. Bohn, 1852).

WHORF, BENJAMIN LEE, 'Languages and Logic', *Language, Thought, and Reality*, ed. J. B. Carroll (Cambridge, Mass.: MIT Press, 1956), 240–1.

WIGNER, EUGENE P., 'The Unreasonable Effectiveness of Mathematics in the Natural Sciences', *Communications on Pure and Applied Mathematics*, 13 (1960).

WOLFF, CHRISTIAN, *Philosophia prima sive ontologia*, ed. J. Ecole (Darmstadt: Wissenschaftlache Buchgesellschaft, 1962).

ZIPF, GEORGE K., *Human Behavior and the Principle of Least Effort* (Cambridge, Mass.: Addison-Wesley Press, 1949).

Name Index